Howard Clemens Hillegas

Oom Paul's People

A narrative of the British-Boer troubles in South Africa, with a history of the Boers, the country, and its institutions

Howard Clemens Hillegas

Oom Paul's People
A narrative of the British-Boer troubles in South Africa, with a history of the Boers, the country, and its institutions

ISBN/EAN: 9783744751377

Printed in Europe, USA, Canada, Australia, Japan

Cover: Foto ©ninafisch / pixelio.de

More available books at **www.hansebooks.com**

President Kruger on the piazza of the Executive Mansion, Pretoria.

OOM PAUL'S PEOPLE

A NARRATIVE OF THE BRITISH-BOER TROUBLES
IN SOUTH AFRICA, WITH A HISTORY
OF THE BOERS, THE COUNTRY,
AND ITS INSTITUTIONS

By HOWARD C. HILLEGAS

ILLUSTRATED WITH EIGHT PHOTOGRAPHS
AND A MAP OF SOUTH AFRICA

NEW YORK
D. APPLETON AND COMPANY
1899

PREFACE

AMERICAN enterprises in South Africa, and especially in the Transvaal, have assumed such large proportions in the last five years that the affairs of the country and the people are steadily gaining in interest the land over. As almost all the interest is centred in the Transvaal and the Boers, an unprejudiced opinion of the country and its people may serve to correct some of the many popular misconceptions concerning them. The Boers constitute a nation, and are deserving of the consideration which many writings concerning them fail to display. They have their failings, as many a more powerful nation has, but they also have noble traits. In these pages an effort has been made to describe the Boers as they impressed themselves upon my mind while I associated with them in the farmhouses on the veldt, in the drawing-rooms in the cities, in the chambers of the Government House, and in the mansion of the Executive.

The alleged grievances of the Uitlanders are so complex and multitudinous that a mere enumeration of them would necessitate a separate volume, and consequently they are not touched upon except collectively. As a layman, it is not within my province to discuss the diplomatic features of South African affairs, and I have shown only the moral aspect as it was unfolded to an American whose pride in the Anglo-Saxon race causes him to wish that there were more justice and less venom in the grievances.

To the many South Africans with whose hospitable treatment I was favoured I am deeply and sincerely grateful. Englishmen, Afrikanders, Dutchmen, Boers, and Uitlanders were exceptionally gracious in many ways, and, however they may have differed on local topics, were unanimously courteous in their entertainment of a citizen of the country for which they frequently expressed such great admiration. I am especially indebted to Sir Alfred Milner, the Queen's High Commissioner to South Africa and Governor of Cape Colony, and Sir James Sivewright, the Acting Premier of Cape Colony, for many courtesies and much information; to President S. J. P. Kruger for many kindnesses and a greatly treasured Transvaal flag; to Postmaster-General Van Alphen, Mr. Peter Dillingham, Commissioner of War Smidt, and many other Government officials, for valuable assistance given to me in Pretoria. To those stanch Americans, Mr. Gardner F. Williams, of Kimberley, and Dr. J. Perrott Prince, of Durban, I am indebted for many pleasant excursions and experiences, and finally to my friend Mr. W. M. B. Tuttle, of New York city, for valuable assistance in this work.

HOWARD C. HILLEGAS.

NEW YORK CITY, *September 4, 1899.*

CONTENTS

CHAPTER	PAGE
I.—SOUTH AFRICA OF THE PRESENT TIME	1

Its physical and political divisions—Relations of the races—Progress of the natives—Transvaal's relative position.

II.—THE EARLY HISTORY OF THE BOER RACE . . 25

Early settlement of the Cape—Troubles of the immigrants with the East India Company and the English—The Great Trek—Battles with the natives and the English—Founding of the republic.

III.—THE JOHANNESBURG GOLD FIELDS . . . 64

Discovery of gold—Early days of the field and the influx of foreigners—The origin of the enmity between the Boers and the newcomers—The Jameson raid and its results.

IV.—THE BOER OF TO-DAY 88

His habits and modes of living—His love of family—His religion and patriotism.

V.—PRESIDENT KRUGER 110

Personal description—His long and active career—His public services—Anecdotes of his life—His home life.

VI.—INTERVIEW WITH PRESIDENT KRUGER . . 136

His democracy—Hatred of Mr. Rhodes—Discussion of the Transvaal's position—His opinion of Americans—Why he hates the English—A message to America.

CHAPTER	PAGE
VII.—CECIL JOHN RHODES	159

The ambition of the man—Story of his youth—His many enterprises—Political career—Personality—Anecdotes and incidents of his life—Groote Schuur—His home.

VIII.—THE BOER GOVERNMENT—CIVIL AND MILITARY	191

The executive and legislative branches of the Government—The Raads in session—The state military organization — Mobilizing the army — Commandant-General P. J. Joubert—His services to the republic.

IX.—CAUSES OF PRESENT DISSENSIONS	215

British contempt of the Boers—The suzerainty dispute—The question of the franchise—Campaign of slander.

X.—PREPARATIONS FOR DEFENCE	236

Boers' strong defences—Attitude of the races—The Afrikander Bond—Armed strength of races—England's preparation—Importance of Delagoa Bay.

XI.—AMERICAN INTERESTS IN SOUTH AFRICA	259

American influence—Exports and imports—Leaders of the American colony—American machinery—Prominent part Americans have taken in the development of the country.

XII.—JOHANNESBURG OF TO-DAY	283

Approach to the city—Description of the city—Its characteristics—Its inhabitants.

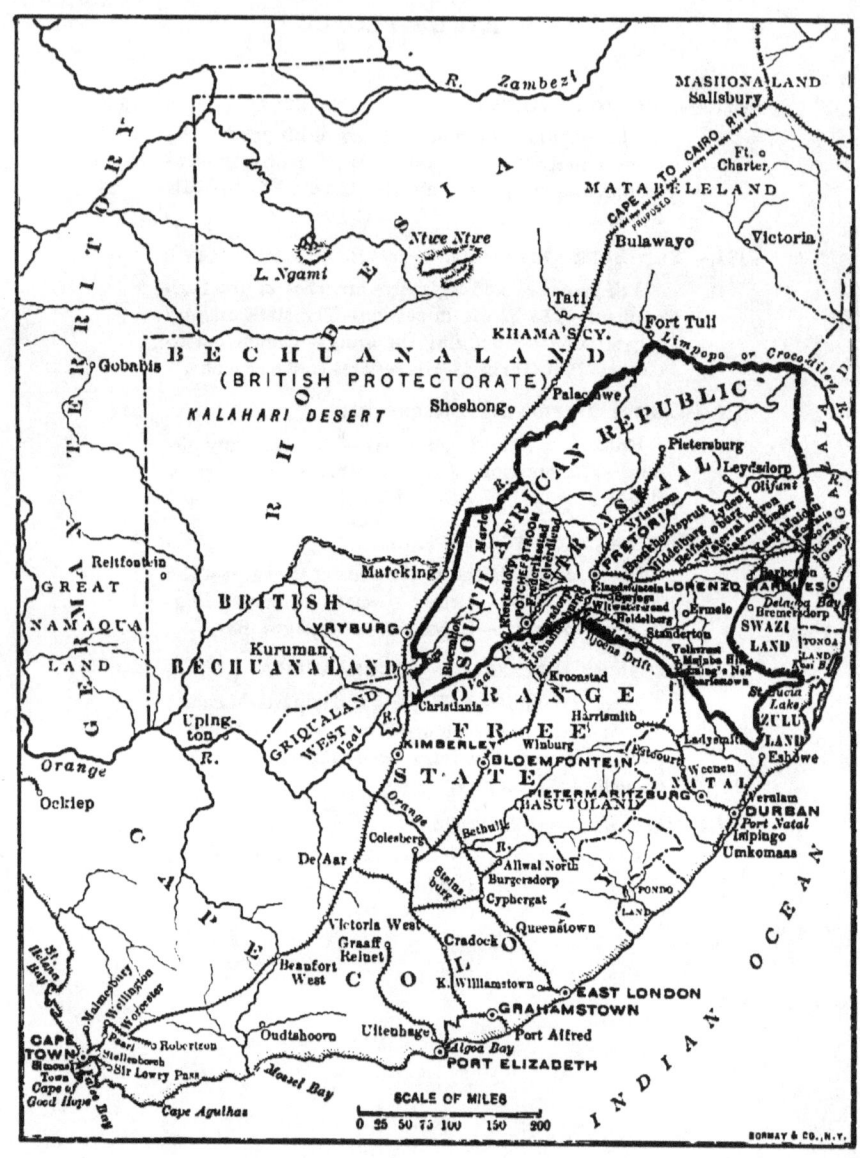

Map of South Africa.

LIST OF ILLUSTRATIONS

	FACING PAGE
President Kruger on the piazza of the Executive Mansion, Pretoria	*Frontispiece*
A band of Zulu warriors in war costume	42
Majuba Hill, where one hundred and fifty Boer volunteers defeated six hundred British soldiers	58
Kirk Street, Pretoria, with the State Church in the distance	98
The Rt. Hon. Cecil J. Rhodes on the piazza of his residence, Groote Schuur, at Rondebosch, near Cape Town	159
Cape Colony Government House, at Cape Town	218
Cape Town and Table Mountain	259
Zulu maidens shaking hands	284
Map of South Africa	x

OOM PAUL'S PEOPLE

CHAPTER I

SOUTH AFRICA OF THE PRESENT TIME

THE population of South Africa may be divided into three great classes of individuals: First, those who are only waiting for the time when they will be able to leave the country—the Uitlanders; second, those who hope that that time may speedily come—the native-born whites; and, third, those who have no hope at all—the negroes.

The white population, south of the Zambezi River, is almost as large as the population of the city of Philadelphia. Half of the population is Boer, or of Dutch extraction, while the remainder consists of the other Afrikanders and the Uitlanders. The Afrikander class comprises those persons who were born in the country but of European descent, while the

Uitlanders are the foreigners who are, for the most part, only temporary residents. The negro population is estimated at five millions, divided into many tribes and scattered over many thousand miles of territory, but united in the common cause of subdued hostility toward the whites.

The discovery and first settlement of South Africa were made about the same time that America was being won from the Indians; but, instead of having a people that united in the one object of making a great and influential nation, South Africa is rent asunder by political intrigue, racial antagonism, and internal jealousies and strife. The Dutch and Boers have their mutual enemies, the Uitlanders; the Cape Colonists are unfriendly with the Natalians, yet unite to a great extent in opposing the Dutch and Boers; while all are the common enemy of the black race.

Strife is incessant in the country, and a unification of interests is impossible so long as the enmity continues. Meanwhile the natural growth and development of the country are retarded, and all classes suffer like consequences.

A man who is capable of healing all the differences and uniting all the classes in a common bond of patriotism will be the saviour of the country, and far greater than Kruger or Rhodes. A fugitive bit of verse that is heard in all parts of South Africa affords a clearer idea of the country than can be given in pages of detailed description. With a few expurgations, the verse is:

> "The rivers of South Africa have no waters,
> The birds no song, the flowers no scent;
> The child you see has no father,
> The whites go free, while the negroes pay the rent."

A person who has derived his impressions of the physical features of the continent of Africa from books generally concludes that it is either a desert or a tropical wilderness throughout. South Africa combines these two features in such a way that the impression need not be entirely shattered, and yet it is not a truthful one.

South Africa is at once a tropical garden, a waterless desert, a fertile plain, and a mountainous wilderness. It has all the distinctions of soil, climate, and physical features that are to be found anywhere in the world, and yet in three hundred years less than half a million persons have found its variety agreeable enough to become permanent residents. Along the coast country, for one hundred miles inland, the territory is as fertile as any in the world, the climate salubrious, and the conditions for settlement most agreeable. Beyond that line is another area of several hundred miles which consists chiefly of lofty tablelike plateaus and forest-covered mountains.

Farther inland is the Great Karroo, a desert of sombre renown, and beyond that the great rolling plains of the Kimberley region, the Orange Free State, and the Transvaal. Here, during the dry season, the earth is covered with brown, lifeless grass, the rays of the sun beat down perpendicularly, and great clouds of yellow dust obscure the horizon. No trees or bushes are seen in a half-thousand-mile journey, the great broad rivers are waterless, and the only live objects are the lone Boer herders and their thirsty flocks.

A month later the rainy season may commence, and then the landscape becomes more animated. Rains, compared with which the heaviest precipitations of the north temperate zone are mere drizzles, continue almost incessantly for weeks; the plain becomes a tropical garden, and the traveller sees some reasons for that part of the earth's creation.

In the midst of these plains, and a thousand miles from the Cape of Good Hope, are the gold mines of the Randt, richer than California and more valuable than the Klondike. The wonder is that they were ever discovered, and almost as marvellous is it that any one should remain there sufficiently long to dig a thousand feet below the surface to secure the hidden wealth. Farther north are the undeveloped countries, Mashonaland and Matabeleland, the great lakes, and the relics of the civilization that is a thousand years older than ours.

According to the American standard, the most uninhabitable part of South Africa is the Transvaal, that inland territory of sun and plain, which has its only redeeming feature in its underground wealth. Had Nature placed her golden treasure in the worthless Kalahari Desert, it would have been of easier access than in the Transvaal, and worthy of a plausible excuse. But, excluding the question of gold, no one except the oppressed Boers ever had the weakest reason for settling in countries so unnatural, unattractive, and generally unproductive as the Transvaal and the Orange Free State.

Cape Colony and Natal, the two British colonies on the coast, are the direct opposites of the Transvaal and the Orange Free State in physical and climatic conditions. The colonies are comfortably settled, the soil is marvellously productive, negro labour is cheap, and everything combines to form the foundation for a great nation.

. Cape Town, the city where every one is continually awaiting the arrival of the next mail steamer from England, and the capital of Cape Colony, is a modern city of fifty thousand inhabitants, mostly English. It was the metropolis of the country until Johannesburg was born in a day, and caused it to become a mere point in transit. The city has electric lights, electric street railways, fine docks, excellent railways into the interior, and all the other attributes of an English city, with the possible exception that it requires a four-weeks' passage to reach London.

It is a city of which Englishmen are proud, for its statue of Queen Victoria is beautiful, the Government society is exclusive, "Tommy Atkins" is there in regiments, and the British flag floats on every staff. Cape Town, too, is the home of the politicians who manage the Colonial Office, which in turn has charge of the South African colonial affairs. Two cable lines lead from South Africa to London, and both dive into the ocean at Cape Town, where live Cecil J. Rhodes, Sir Alfred Milner, and the other politicians who furnish the cablegrams and receive the replies. Farther north on the east coast, about three days' sail around the Cape, is the colony of Natal, peaceful, paradisaical, and proud. Taken by conquest from the Zulus a half century ago, it has already distanced its four-times-older competitor, Cape Colony, in almost all things that pertain to the development of a country. Being fifteen hundred miles farther from London than Cape Town, it has escaped the political swash of that city, and has been able to plough its own path in the sea of colonial settlement.

Almost all of Natal is included in the fertile coast territory, and consequently has been able to offer excellent inducements to intending settlers. The majority of these have been Scotchmen of sturdy stock, and these have established a diminutive Scotland in South Africa, and one that is a model for the entire continent. Within the last year the colony has annexed the adjoining country of the Zulus, which, even if it accomplishes nothing more practical, increases the size of the colony. Durban, the entry port of the colony, is the Newport of South Africa, as well as its Colorado Springs. Its wide, palm-and-flower-fringed streets, its 'ricksha Zulus, its magnificent suburbs, and its healthful climate combine to make Durban the finest residence city on the Dark Continent. Pietermaritzburg, the capital of the colony, on the other hand, has nothing but its age to commend it. The colony produces vast quantities of coffee, tea, sugar, and fruits, almost all of which is marketed in Johannesburg, in the Transvaal, which is productive of nothing but gold and strife.

The Orange Free State, which, with the Transvaal, form the only non-English states in South Africa, also lies in the plain or veldt district, and is of hardly any commercial importance. Three decades ago it found itself in almost the same situation with England as the Transvaal is to-day, but, unlike the South African republic, feared to demand its rights from the British Government. At that time the Kimberley diamond mines were discovered on acknowledged Free State soil. England purchased an old native chief's claims, which had been disallowed by a court of arbitration, and pushed them as its own. The Free State was weak, and agreed to forfeit its claim in return for a sum of four hundred and fifty thousand dollars. The mines, now owned by a syndicate, of which Cecil J. Rhodes is the head, have yielded more than four hundred million dollars' worth of diamonds since the Free State ceded them to England for less than half a million dollars.

The natives, who less than one hundred

years ago ruled the whole of South Africa with the exception of a small fraction of Cape Colony and several square miles on the east coast, have been relegated by the advances of civilization, until now they hold only small territories, or reservations, in the different colonies and republics. They are making slow progress in the arts of civilization, except in Cape Colony, where, under certain conditions, they are allowed to exercise the franchise, and on the whole have profited but little by the advent of the whites, notwithstanding the efforts of missionaries and governments. They smart under the treatment of the whites, who, having forcibly taken their country from them, now compel them to pay rental for the worst parts of the country, to which they are circumscribed, and to wear brass tags, with numbers, like so many cattle.

Comparatively few natives work longer than three months of the year, and would not do that except for the fear of punishment for non-payment of hut taxes. With the exception of those who are employed in the towns and cities, the negroes wear the same scanty costumes of their forefathers, and follow the same customs and practices. Witchcraft and superstition still rule the minds of the majority, and the former is practised in all its cruel hideousness in many parts of the country, although prohibited by law.

The sale of rum, the great American "civilizer" of the Indians, is also prohibited in all the states and colonies, but it frequently is the cause of rebellious and intertribal wars. Notwithstanding the generous use of "dum-dum" bullets in the recent campaigns against the negroes, and the score of other agents of civilization which carry death to the natives, the black population has increased greatly since the control of the country has been taken from them. In Natal, particularly, the increase in the Zulu population has been most threatening to the continued safety of that energetic colony. The Colonial Office, through generous and humanitarian motives, has fostered the development of the native by every means possible. No rabbit warren or pheasant hatchery was ever conducted on a more modern basis.

Everything that the most enthusiastic founder of a new colony could do to increase the population of his dominion is in practice in Natal. Polygamy is not prohibited, and is indulged in to the full extent of the natives' purchasing ability. Innumerable magistrates and police are scattered throughout the country to prevent internecine warfare and petty quarrels. The Government protects the Zulu from external war, pestilence, and famine. King Tshaka's drastic method of recurring to war in order to keep down the surplus population has been succeeded by the Natal incubation scheme, which has proved so successful that the colony's native population is fourfold greater than it was when Tshaka ruled the country. The situation is a grave one for the colony, whose fifty thousand whites would be like so many reeds in a storm if the half million Zulus should break the bonds in which they have been held since the destruction of Cetewayo's army in the recent Zulu war.

The only tribe of natives that has made any progress as a body is that which is under the leadership of King Khama, the most intelligent negro in South Africa. Before his conversion to Christianity, Khama was at the head of one of the most bloodthirsty, polygamous, and ignorant tribes in the country. Since that event he has been the means of converting his entire tribe of wild and treacherous negroes to Christianity, has abandoned polygamy and tribal warfare, and has established a government, schools, churches, and commercial enterprises. In addition to all his other good works, he has assisted Great Britain in pacifying many belligerent tribes, and has become England's greatest friend in South Africa.

Khama is the paramount chief of the Bawangwato tribe, whose territory is included in the British Bechuanaland protectorate, situated about one thousand miles due north from Cape Town. There are about fifteen thousand men, women, and children in the kingdom, and every one of that number tries to emulate the noble examples set by their king, whom all adore. The country and climate of Khama's Kingdom, as it is officially called, are magnificent, and so harmless and inoffensive are the people that the traveller is less exposed to attacks by marauders than he is in the streets along New York's water front.

Many Europeans have settled in Khama's Kingdom for the purpose of mining and trading, and these have assisted in placing the Bawangwatos on a plane of civilization far above and beyond that attained by any other negro nation or tribe in the country. A form of government has been adopted, and is carried out with excellent results. The laws, which must be sanctioned by the British Government before they can be put in force, are transgressed with an infrequency that puts to shame many a country of boasted ancient civilization. Theft is unknown and murders are unheard of, while drunkenness is to be seen only when a white man smuggles liquor into the country. A public-school system has been introduced, and has resulted in giving a fairly good education to all the youth. Even music is taught, and several of the brass bands that have been organized compare favourably with such as are found in many rural communities in America.

Well-regulated farms and cattle ranches are located in all parts of the territory, and in most instances are profitably and wisely conducted. The negroes have abandoned the use of beads and skins almost entirely, and now pattern after Europeans in the matter of clothing. Witchcraft and kindred vices have not been practised for fifty years, and only the older members of the tribe know that such practices existed. The remarkable man to whom is due the honour of having civilized an entire nation of heathen is now about eighty years old. He speaks the English language fluently, and writes it much more legibly than his distinguished friend Cecil Rhodes.

Khama is about six feet in height, well proportioned, and remarkably strong despite his great age. His skin is not black, but of that dark copper colour borne by negro chiefs of the royal line. He has the bearing of a nobleman, and is extremely polite and affable in his treatment of visitors. He is well informed on all current topics, and his knowledge of South African men and affairs is wonderful. In his residence, which is constructed of stone and on English lines, Khama has all the accessories necessary for a civilized man's comfort. He has a library of no small size, a piano for his grandchildren, a folding bed for himself, and, not least of all, an American carriage of state.

It is a strange anomaly that the Boers, a pastoral people exclusively, should have settled in a section of the earth where Nature has two of her richest storehouses. Both the Kimberley diamond mines and the Witwatersrandt gold mines, each the richest deposit of its kind discovered thus far, were found where the Boers were accustomed to graze their herds and flocks. It would seem as if Nature had influenced the Boers to settle above her treasures, and protect them from the attacks of nations and men who are not satisfied with the products of the earth's surface, but must delve below.

This circumstance has been both fortunate and unfortunate for the Boer people. It has laid them open to the attacks of covetous nations, which have not been conducive to a restful existence, but it has made their country what it is to-day—the source from which all the other South African states draw their means of support. The Transvaal is the main wheel in the South African machinery. Whenever the Transvaal is disturbed, Cape Colony, Natal, and the Orange Free State are similarly affected, because they are dependent upon the Boer country for almost their breath of life. When the Transvaal flourishes, South Africa flourishes, and when the Transvaal suffers, then the rest of the country is in dire straits.

Before the diamond and gold mines were discovered, South Africa was practically a cipher in the commercial world. The country exported nothing, because it produced no more than was needed for home consumption, and it could import nothing because it was too poor to pay for imported goods. The discovery of the diamond mines twenty-five years ago caused the country to be in a flourishing condition for several years, but the formation of the De Beers syndicate ended it by monopolizing the industry, and consequently starving the individual miners. The country was about to relapse into its former condition when the Transvaal mines were unearthed. No syndicate having been strong enough to consolidate all the mines and monopolize the industry, as was done at Kimberley, and the Boers having resisted all efforts to defraud them out of the valuable part of their country, as had happened to the Orange Free State Boers, the Transvaal soon attained the paramount position in the country, and has retained it since.

Until Lobengula, the mighty native chief of the regions west of the Transvaal, was subdued and his country taken from him, the British empire builders were limited in their field of endeavour, because the Transvaal was the only pass through which an entry could be made into the vast Central African region. When Lobengula's power yielded to British arms, the Transvaal became useless as the key to Central Africa, but, by means of its great mineral wealth, became of so much greater and more practical importance that it really was the entire South Africa.

The Witwatersrandt,* the narrow strip of gold-bearing soil which extends for almost one hundred miles east and west through the Transvaal, is the lever which moves the entire coun-

---

* Witwatersrandt is the name given to the high ridge in the southern part of the Transvaal, which is the watershed between the Atlantic and Indian Oceans. The word means "white water ridge," and is commonly abridged to "The Randt."

try. In the twelve years since its discovery it has been transformed from a grass-covered plain into a territory that is filled with cities, towns, and villages. Where the Boer farmer was accustomed to graze his cattle are hundreds of shafts that lead to the golden caverns below, and the trail of the ox-team is now the track of the locomotive and the electric cars.

The farmer's cottage has developed into the city of Johannesburg, the home of more than one hundred thousand persons and the metropolis of a continent. All the roads in South Africa lead to Johannesburg, and over them travels every one who enters the country either for pleasure or business. The Transvaal is the only great producer of money, as well as the only great consumer, and consequently all other communities in the country are dependent upon it for whatever money it chooses to yield to them. The natural conditions are such, however, that, while the Transvaal has almost all the money in South Africa, it is compelled to support Cape Colony, Natal, and the Orange Free State like so many poor relations.

The Transvaal, being an inland state, is the feeding ground of those states which are located between it and the sea. Every ton of foreign freight that enters the Transvaal through Cape Colony is subject to high customs duties and abnormal freight rates. The railway and the customs house being under the same jurisdiction, it will readily be seen to what extent Cape Colony derives its revenues from the Transvaal commerce. The Orange Free State again taxes the freight before allowing it to pass through its territory. The third tax, which makes the total far greater than the original cost of the freight, is added by the Transvaal Government. Certain classes of freight shipped from Europe are taxed by the steamship line, the Cape Colony Railroad, the Transvaal Railroad, and with Cape Colony, Orange Free State, and Transvaal customs duties.

This vast expenditure is borne by the consumers in the Transvaal, who are compelled to pay from three to five times as much for rent and food as is paid in England or America. Cape Colony, in particular, has been fattening upon the Transvaal. The Government railroads in one year showed a profit of more than eight per cent. upon the capital invested, after accounting for the great losses incurred with unprofitable branch lines, showing that the main line to the Transvaal must have produced a profit of from fifteen to twenty per cent. The customs duties collected by Cape Colony on almost all freight in transit is five per cent. of its value. The inhabitants of the Transvaal are obliged to pay these large amounts, and are so much poorer while the Cape Colony Government preys upon them. The Transvaal Government receives none of this revenue except that from its customs, which is insufficient for its expenses.

After having grown wealthy in this manner, the colony of Natal has recently become conscience-smitten, and allows freight to pass in transit without taxing it with customs duties. The Government owns the railroad, and is content with the revenue it secures from the Transvaal freight without twice preying upon the republic.

Not only have the colonial governments profited by the existence of the gold mines in the Transvaal, but the cities, towns, and individuals of Cape Colony, Natal, and the Orange Free State have also had a period of unparalleled prosperity. Although the natural resources of the Transvaal are very great, they have not been developed, and the other colonies which have been developed along those lines are supplying the deficit. Almost every ounce of food consumed in the Transvaal arrives from over the border. Natal and Cape Colony supply the corn, wheat, cattle, and sugar, and, having a monopoly of the supply close at hand, can command any price for their commodities.

Industries have grown up in Natal and Cape Colony that are entirely dependent upon the Transvaal for their existence, and their establishment has been responsible for much of the recent growth of the population of the colonies. The large sugar factories and fruit farms in Natal have the only market for their products in the Transvaal, and the large farms and vineyards in Cape Colony supply the same demand. The ports of Durban, Port Elizabeth, and East London, as well as Cape Town, are important only as forwarding stations for goods going or coming from the Transvaal, and but for that Godsend they would still be the listless cities that they were before the discovery of gold on the Randt. Owing to the lack of raw material, the cities have no large factories and industries such as are found even in small American towns, and consequently the inhabitants are obliged to depend upon the traffic with the interior. Notwithstanding this condition of affairs, which causes Natal and Cape Colony to be commercial weaklings, swayed by the Transvaal tide, the colonists are continually harassing the Government of the republic by laws and suggestions. The republic's mote is always bigger than the colonies' own, and the strife is never-ending.

The Transvaal is a country of such enormous value that it has attracted, and will continue to attract, investors from all parts of the earth. The gold production, in the opinion of the first experts on the Randt, will rapidly reach one hundred and twenty-five million dollars a year. It already yields one hundred million a year, or more than a third of the world's production, of which the United States is credited with less than seventy-five million. The very fact of that production, and the world being enriched to that extent, will provide the money for further enterprises. So long as the gold supply continues to appear inexhaustible, and mines continue to pay dividends ranging from one to one hundred and fifty per cent., so long will the Transvaal remain supreme in the commerce and finance of South Africa.

CHAPTER II

THE EARLY HISTORY OF THE BOER RACE

THE early history of the Boers is contemporaneous with that of the progress of white man's civilization at the Cape of Good Hope. The two are interwoven to such an extent and for so long a time that it is well-nigh impossible to separate them. In order to give an unwearisome history of the modern Boer's ancestors, a general outline of the settlement of the Cape will suffice.

The history of the Boers of South Africa has its parallel in that of the early Pilgrims who landed at Plymouth Rock and their descendants. The comparison favours the latter, it is true, but the conditions which confronted the early Boers were so much less favourable that their lack of realization may easily be accounted for. In the early part of the seventeenth century the progenitors of the

Boers and the Pilgrims left their continental homes to seek freedom from religious tyranny on foreign shores.

The boat load of Pilgrims left England to come to America and found the freedom they sought. About the same time a small number of Dutch and Huguenot refugees from France departed from Holland for similar reasons, and decided to seek their fortunes and religious freedom at the Cape of Good Hope. There they found the liberty they desired, and, like the Pilgrims, assiduously set to work to clear the land and institute the works of a civilized community.

The experiences of the two widely separated colonists appear painfully similar, although to them they were undoubtedly preferable to the persecutions inflicted upon them in their native countries. The Pilgrims were constantly harassed by the savage Indians; the Dutch and Huguenots at the Cape had treacherous Hottentots and Bushmen to contend against. Although probably ignorant of each other's existence, the two parties conducted their affairs on similar lines and reached a common result—a good local government and a reasonable state of material prosperity.

The little South African settlement became of recognised importance in the later years of the century, when it was made the halfway station of all ships going to and returning from the East Indies. The necessity for such a station was the foundation of the growth of the settlement at Table Bay, which is only a short distance from the southernmost extremity of the continent, and the increase in population came as a natural sequence.

The Dutch East India Settlement, as it was officially called, attracted hundreds of immigrants. The reports of a salubrious climate, good soil, and, more than all, the promised religious toleration, were the allurements that brought more immigrants from Holland, Germany, and France. Cape Town even then was one of the most important ports in the world, owing to its great strategic value and to the fact that it was about the only port where vessels making the long trip to the East Indies could secure even the scantiest supplies.

The provisioning of ships was responsible, in no small degree, for the growth of Cape Town and the coincident increase in immigration.

When all the available land between Table Mountain and Table Bay was settled, the new arrivals naturally took up the land to the northward, and drove the bellicose natives before them. Like their Pilgrim prototypes, they instituted military organizations to cope with the natives, and they were not infrequently called upon for active duty against them. It was owing to this savage disposition of the natives that the settlers confined their endeavours to the vicinity of Table Bay.

When immigrants became more numerous and land increased in value, the pilgrims of more daring disposition proceeded inland, and soon carried the northeastern boundary of the settlement close to the Orange River. The soil around Table Bay was extremely rich, but farther inland it became barren and, by reason of the many lofty table-lands, almost uninhabitable. The Bushmen, too, were constantly attacking the encroaching settlers, whose lives were filled with anything but thoughts of safety, and high in the northern side of Table Mountain is to be seen to-day an old-time fort that was erected by the settlers to ward off natives' attacks upon Cape Town.

The Dutch East India Company, which controlled the settlement, looked with disfavour upon the enlargement of the original boundary of the colony, and attempted to enforce laws preventing such action. The settlers in the outlying district felt that they owed no allegiance to the laws of the colony in which they did not live, and refused to obey the company's mandates. Then followed a long-drawn-out controversy between the settlers and the East India Company, which resembled in many respects the differences between England and her American colony.

It was during this period of oppression that the settlers of the Cape of Good Hope first exhibited the betokening signs of a nation. The communities of Hollanders, Germans, and French were constantly in such close communication with one another that each lost its distinguishing marks and adopted the new manners and customs which were their collective coinage. They suffered the same indignities at the hands of the East India Company, and naturally their sympathies drew them into a closer bond of fellowship, so that almost all national and racial differences were wiped out.

Never in the history of South Africa were all things so favourable for the establishment of a truly Afrikander nation and government. A leader was all that was necessary to throw off the yoke of continental control, but none was forthcoming.

At this propitious time the Napoleonic wars in Europe resulted so disastrously for France that she was compelled to cede to England the South African settlement, which had been acquired with the annexation of Holland, and the settlers believed their hour of deliverance from tyranny had arrived. They hailed the coming of the British forces with hopes for the improvement of their conditions, fondly believing that the British could treat them with no greater severity than that which they had suffered under the rule of the Dutch Company.

But their hopes were short-lived after the British garrison occupied Cape Town, and they soon learned that they had escaped from one kind of torment and oppression only to be burdened with another more harassing. The British administrators found a friendly people, eager to become British subjects, and, by exercise of undue authority, quickly transformed them into desperate enemies of British rule. The American colonies had but a short time before taught British colonial statesmen a dire lesson, but it was not applied to the South African colony, and the mistake has never been remedied.

Had the lesson learned in America been applied at that time, British rule would now be supreme in South Africa, and the two republics which are the eyesore of every Englishman in the country would probably never have come into existence. The British administrators ruled the colony as they had been taught in London, and allowed no local impediments to swerve them. The result of this method of government was that the Boer settlers, who had opinions of their own, became bitterly opposed to the British rule. The administrators attempted to coerce the Boers, and formulated laws which were meat to the newly arrived English immigrants and poison to the old settlers.

One of the indirect causes of the first Boer uprising against the British Government at the Cape was the slavery question. In the Transvaal there is a national holiday—March 6th—to commemorate the uprising of 1816, and it is known throughout the country as "Slagter's Nek Day." To the Boers it is a day of sad memory, and the recurrence of it does not soften their enmity of the English nation.

In October, 1815, a Boer farmer named Frederick Bezuidenhout was summoned to appear in a local court to answer a charge of maltreating a native. The Boer refused to obey the summons, and, with a sturdy native, awaited the arrival of the Government authorities in a cave near his home. A lieutenant named Rousseau and twenty soldiers found the Boer and the native in the cave, and demanded their surrender. Bezuidenhout refused to surrender, and he was almost instantly killed.

When the news of his death reached his friends they became greatly aroused, and, arming themselves, vowed to expel the English "tyrants" from the country. The English soldiers captured five of the leaders, and on March 6, 1816, hanged them on the same scaffold at Slagter's Nek, a name afterward given to the locality because of the bungling work of the hangmen and the ghastly scenes presented when the scaffold fell to the ground, bearing with it the half-dead prisoners.

The story of this event in the Boer history is as familiar to the Dutch schoolboy as that of the Boston Tea-Party is to the American lad, and its repetition never fails to arouse a Boer audience to the highest degree of anger.

The primal cause of the departure of the Boers from Cape Colony, or the "Great Trek," * as it is popularly known, was the ill treatment which they received from the Brit-

---

* To trek is to travel from place to place in ox-wagons. A trek generally refers to an organized migration of settlers to another part of the country.

ish administration in connection with the emancipation of their slaves and the depredations of hordes of thieving native tribes. The Boers had agreed about 1830 to emancipate all their slaves, and they had received from the British Government promises of ample compensation.

After the slaves had been freed, and the majority of the Boer farmers had become bankrupt by the proceeding, the Government offered less than half the promised compensation. The Boers naturally and indignantly refused to accept less than the amounts England had promised of her own free will. The Boers felt sorely aggrieved, but, being in the minority in the colony, could secure no redress. Several years after the slaves had been freed great hordes of thieving natives swept across the frontiers, and in several months inflicted these losses upon the farmers: 706 farmhouses partially or totally destroyed by fire; 60 farm wagons destroyed; 5,713 horses, 112,000 head of cattle, and 162,000 sheep stolen.

The value of the property destroyed and stolen by the blacks amounted to almost two million dollars. Much of the live stock was recovered by the Boer farmers, who had the boldness to pursue the robbers into their mountain fastnesses, but the Government did not allow them to hold even such cattle as they identified as having been driven away by the natives, but compelled them to yield all to the Government. When they asked for compensation for restoring ,the property to the Government, the Boers received such a promise from the governor, D'Urban; but Lord Glenelg, the British colonial secretary, vetoed the suggestion, and informed the Boers that their conduct in recovering the stolen property was outrageous and unworthy of English subjects.

Even Boer disposition, inured as it was to all kinds of unrighteousness, could not fail to take notice of this crowning insult. They consulted among themselves; and it was decided to leave the colony where they had suffered so many wrongs. Accordingly, in the spring of 1835 they sacrificed their farms at whatever prices they could secure for them, and announced to Lieutenant-Governor Stockenstrom their intention of departing to another section of the country.

To be certain that they would be free from British interference, the Boer leaders applied to the lieutenant-governor for his opinion on the subject, and he informed them that they were free to leave the colony, and that as soon as they stepped across the border England ceased to be their master. Later, Englishmen have sagely declared that the Boers having once been British subjects always remained such, whether they lived on British or Transvaal soil. The objects of the expedition were set forth in a document published in 1837 by Piet Retief, its leader. It reads, in part, as follows:

"We despair of saving the colony from those evils which threaten it by the turbulent and dishonest conduct of native vagrants who are allowed to infest the country in every part; nor do we see any prospect of peace or happiness for our children in a country thus distracted by internal commotions.

"We complain of the continual system of plunder which we have for years endured from the Kaffirs and other coloured classes, and particularly by the last invasion of the colony, which has desolated the frontier districts and ruined most of the inhabitants.

"We complain of the unjustifiable odium which has been cast upon us by interested and dishonest persons under the name of religion, whose testimony is believed in England, to the exclusion of all evidence in our favour, and we can foresee as a result of this prejudice nothing but the total ruin of the country.

"We are now leaving the fruitful land of our birth, in which we have suffered enormous losses and continual vexations, and are about to enter a strange and dangerous territory; but we go with a firm reliance on an all-seeing, just, and merciful God, whom we shall always fear and humbly endeavour to obey."

The first "trekking" party, or the "Voortrekkers," consisted of about two hundred persons under the leadership of Andries Hendrik Potgieter. These crossed the Orange River and settled in that part of the country now known as the Orange Free State. This party had many battles with the natives, but succeeded in securing a level although not particularly arable stretch of land near Thaba'ntshu for settlement.

In August, 1836, after remaining a short time in the neighbourhood of Thaba'ntshu, a number of the settlers became dissatisfied with their location and "trekked" farther north toward the Vaal River, which is the present northern boundary of the Orange Free State. Before they had proceeded a great distance they were attacked by the Matabele natives under Chief Moselekatse, and fifty of their number were slain.

When the news of the slaughter reached the main body of the settlers a "laager," or improvised fort, was formed by locking together the fifty big transport wagons that had been brought from Cape Colony. Behind these the men, women, and children fought side by side against the innumerable Matabeles, and after a desperate battle succeeded in defeating them. The natives captured and drove away about ten thousand head of cattle and sheep —almost the entire wealth of the settlers.

THE EARLY HISTORY OF THE BOER RACE 39

The settlement, however, increased rapidly in population, and, several years after the first Boers arrived there, application was made for English protection. It was granted to them, but was withdrawn again in 1854, when the British colonial secretary decided that England had more African land than was desirable. The Boers begged to be retained as an English colony, but in vain, and the fifteen thousand inhabitants were compelled to establish a government of their own, which is to-day embodied in that of the Orange Free State.

Since that memorable day in 1854, when the British flag was hauled down from the flagstaff at the Bloemfontein fort, both the British and the Boers have had revulsions of feeling. The British regret that their flag is absent from the fort, and the Boers will yield their lives before they ever allow it to be raised again.

The second expedition, and the one which comprised the founders of the South African Republic, departed from Cape Colony in the fall of 1835, with no fixed destination in view, but with a general idea to settle somewhere outside the realm of British influence. The "trekkers" were under the leadership of Piet Retief, a man of considerable wealth and executive ability, who determined to lead them across the untravelled Dragon Mountain, in the east of the colony.

In this party were three families of Krugers, and among them the present President of the South African Republic, then a boy of ten years. After many skirmishes with the natives, Retief and his followers reached Port Natal, the site of the present beautiful city of Durban, where they were welcomed by the members of the English settlement who had established themselves on the edge of Zululand as an independent organization. The handful of British immigrants were overjoyed to have this addition to the forces which were necessary to hold the natives in subjection, and they induced the majority of the Boers to settle in the vicinity of Port Natal.

Retief and his leaders were pleased with the location and the richness of the soil, and finally determined to remain there if the native chiefs could be induced to enter into treaties transferring all rights to the soil. Dingaan, a warlike native, was the chief of the tribes surrounding Port Natal, and to him Retief applied for the grant of territory which was to be the future home of the several thousand "trekkers" who had by that time journeyed over Dragon Mountain. Retief and his party of seventy, and thirty native servants, reached Dingaan's capital in January, 1838, and took with them as a peace-offering several hundred head of cattle which had been stolen from Dingaan by another tribe and recovered by Retief.

Dingaan treated the Boers with great courtesy, and profusely thanked them for recovering his stolen cattle. After several interviews he ceded to the Boers the large territory from the Tugela to the Umzimvubu River, from the Dragon Mountain to the sea. This territory included almost the entire colony of Natal, as now constituted, and was one of the richest parts of South Africa.

On February 4, 1838, when the treaty had been signed and the Boer leaders were being entertained by the chief in his hut, a typical massacre by the natives was enacted. At a signal from Dingaan, which is recorded as having been "Bulala abatagati" ("Slay the white devils!"), the Zulus sprang upon the unarmed Boers and massacred the seventy men with assegais and clubs before they could make the slightest resistance.

Frenzied by the sight of the white men's blood, the Zulu chieftain gathered his hordes in warlike preparation, and determined to drive all the white settlers out of the country. A large "impi," or war party, was despatched to attack and exterminate the remaining whites in their camps on the Tugela and Bushmans Rivers. These latter, while anxiously awaiting Retief's return, were in no fear of hostilities, and the men for the most part were absent from their camps on hunting trips.

The "impi" swept down upon the camps by night, and murder of the foulest description prevailed. The Zulus spared none; men, women, and children, cattle, goats, sheep, and dogs—all fell under the ruthless assegais in the hands of the treacherous savages. In the confusion and darkness a few of the Boers escaped,

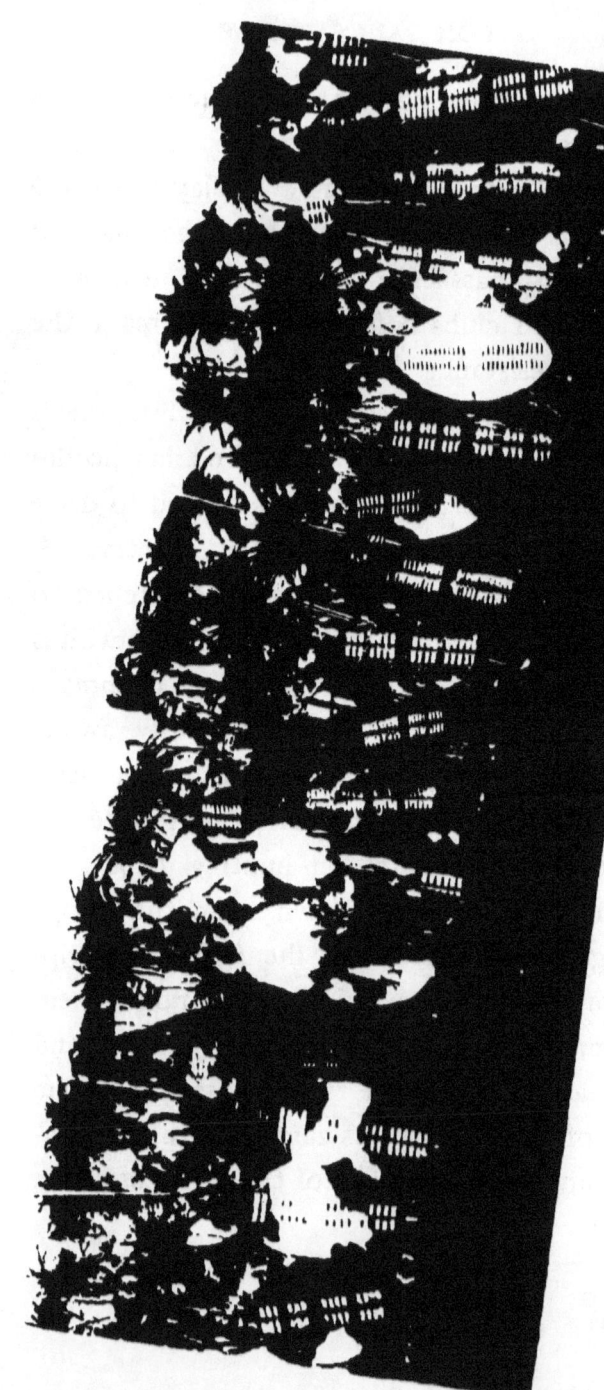

A band of Zulu warriors in war costume.

among them having been the Pretorius and Rensburg families, which have since been high in the councils of the Boer nation. Fourteen men and boys took refuge on a hill now called Rensburg Kop, and held their assailants at bay while they improvised a "laager."

When their ammunition was almost expended and their spirit exhausted, a white man on horseback was observed in the rear of the Zulu warriors. The hard-pressed emigrants signalled to him, and his ready mind, strained to the utmost tension, grasped the situation at a glance. He fearlessly turned his horse and rode to the abandoned wagons, almost a mile away, to secure some of the ammunition that had been left behind by the Boers when they were attacked by the Zulus. He loaded himself and his horse with powder and ball from the wagons, and with a courage that has never been surpassed rode headlong through the Zulu battle lines and bore to the beleaguered Boers the means of their subsequent salvation. That night the fearless rider assisted the fourteen Boers in routing the

Zulus, and when morning dawned not a single living Zulu was to be seen.

The hero of that ride was Marthinus Oosthuyse, and his fame in South Africa rivals that of Paul Revere in American history. With the coming of the day the scattered emigrants congregated in a large "laager," and for several days were engaged in beating off the attacks of the unsatiated Zulus. Wives, daughters, and sweethearts served the ammunition to the men, and with hatchets and clubs aided them in the uneven struggle.

After the Zulus' spirit had been broken and they commenced to retreat, the gallant pioneers, their strength now increased by the addition of many stragglers, pursued their late assailants and killed hundreds of them. The town of Weenen, in Natal, takes its name from the weeping of the Boers for their dead. Rightly was it named, for no less than six hundred of the emigrants were massacred by the Zulus in the neighbourhood of the present site of the town.

While this massacre was in progress Dingaan and another part of his vast and well-trained army set out to wreak destruction upon the main body of the Boers which was still encamped upon the Dragon Mountain waiting for the return of Retief and his party. When the news of the massacre reached the main body, Pieter Uys and Potgieter hastened to re-enforce their distressed countrymen. They were not molested on the way, and had ample time to marshal all the Boer forces in the country and make preparations for vengeance upon the savages.

A force of three hundred and fifty men was raised, and this set out in the month of April, 1838, to attack Dingaan in his stronghold. The Zulu army was encountered near the King's "Great Place." The small army of Boers rode to within twenty yards of the van of the Zulus and then opened a steady and deadly fire. The savage weapons were no match for the poor yet superior firearms of the Boers, and in a short time Dingaan's army was in full retreat. In pursuing them the Boers became separated and had great difficulty in fighting their way back to the main camp.

The story of how Pieter Uys was wounded by an assegai, and how his son, in endeavouring to save him, was pierced by a spear, is one of the noblest examples of heroism in the annals of South Africa. There were several more skirmishes with the Zulus, but the battle that broke the strength of the tribe was fought on December 16, 1838. There were but four hundred and sixty Boers in the army that attacked Dingaan's army of twelve thousand, but the attack was so minutely planned and so admirably executed that the smaller force overwhelmed the greater and won the victory, which is annually observed on "Dingaan's Day."

The Boers lay fortified in a "laager," and with unusual fortitude withstood the terrific onslaughts of the thousands of Zulus. Finally a cavalry charge of two hundred Boers created a panic in the Zulu army, and they retreated precipitously toward the Blood River, which was so named because its waters literally ran red with the life fluid of four hundred warriors who were shot on its banks or while attempting to ford it. On that day three thousand Zulus perished, and Dingaan made his ruin still more complete by burning his capital and hiding with his straggling army in the wilderness beyond the Tugela River.

After these grave experiences the Boer settlers believed themselves to be the rightful owners of the country which they had first sought to obtain by peaceful methods and afterward been compelled to take by sterner ones. But when they reached Port Natal they found that the British Government had taken possession of the country, and had issued a manifesto that the immigrant Boers were to be treated as a conquered race, and that their arms and ammunition should be confiscated.

To the Boers, who had just made the country valuable by clearing it of the Zulus, this high-handed action of the British Government had the appearance of persecution, and they naturally resented it, although they were almost powerless to oppose it by force of arms.

The Boer leader, Commandant-General Pretorius, who had been chosen by the first "Volksraad"—a governing body elected while the journey from Cape Colony to Natal was being made—led a number of his countrymen to the outskirts of Durban and formed a camp near that of the British garrison. He sent a message to Captain Smith, the commander of the British force of several hundred soldiers, and demanded the surrender of his position. In reply Smith led one hundred and fifty of his soldiers in a moonlight attack on the Boer forces and was completely routed.

The Boers then besieged Durban for twenty-six days and killed many of the English soldiers, but on the twenty-seventh day a schooner load of soldiers from Cape Colony augmented the forces of Captain Smith, and Pretorius was compelled to relinquish his efforts to secure control of the territory that his countrymen had a short time previously won from the Zulus.

Disheartened by their successive failures to secure a desirable part of the country wherein they might settle, the Boers again "trekked" northward over the Dragon Mountain. There they occupied the territory south of the Vaal River which had a short time previously been deserted by Potgieter and his party, who had journeyed northward with the intention of joining the Portuguese colony at Delagoa Bay, on the Indian Ocean.

These pilgrims were attacked by the deadly fever of the Portuguese country, and after remaining a short time in that region moved again and settled in different localities in the northern part of the territory now included in the South African Republic. Moselekatse and his Matabele warriors having been driven out of the country by the other "trekking" parties, the extensive region north of the Vaal River was then in undisputed possession of the Boers.

The farmers who left Cape Colony in 1835 and 1836 in different parties and after various vicissitudes settled across the Vaal were less than sixteen thousand in number, and were scattered over a large area of territory. The nature of the country and the enmity of the leaders of the parties prevented a close union among them, although a legislative assembly, called a "Volksraad," was established after much disorder. The four principal "trekking" parties had sought four of the most fertile spots in the newly discovered territory, and established the villages of Utrecht, Lydenburg, Potchefstrom, and Zoutpansberg.

When the Volksraad was found to be inadequate to meet the requirements of the situation these villages were transformed into republics, each with a government independent of the others. The government of the limited areas of land occupied by the four republics was fairly successful, but the surrounding territory became a practical no-man's-land, where roamed the worst criminals of the country and hundreds of detached bands of marauding natives.

The Boers imposed a labour tax upon all the natives who lived in the territory claimed by the four republics, and for a period of ten years the taxes were paid without a murmur. About that time, however, the native tribes had recovered from the great losses inflicted upon them by the emigrant farmers, and they were numerous enough to make an armed resistance to the demands of the governments. White women and children were massacred and property was destroyed at every opportunity.

For purposes of self-preservation the four republics decided to unite the governments under one head, and, after many disputes and disorders, succeeded, in May, 1864, in forming a single republic, with Marthinus Wessel Pretorius as President, and Paul Kruger as commandant-general of the army.

Ten months after the organization of the republic the Barampula tribe and a number of lawless Europeans rebelled against the authority of the Government, and Kruger was obliged to attempt their subjugation. Owing to a lack of ammunition and funds, he failed to end the rebellion, and as a result the Boers were compelled to withdraw from a large part of the territory they had occupied. Up to this time the Boers had not been interfered with by the Government of Cape Colony, but another tribal rebellion that followed the Barampula disturbance led to the establishment of a court of arbitration, in which the English governor of Natal figured as umpire.

The result of the arbitration was that the rebellious tribes were awarded their independence, and that a large part of the Boers' territory was taken from them. The emigrant farmers who had settled the country maintained that President Pretorius was responsible for the loss of territory and compelled him to resign, after which the Rev. Thomas François Burgers, a shrewd but just clergyman-lawyer, was elected head of the republic. Burgers believed that the republic was destined to become a power of world-wide magnitude, and instantly used his position to attain that object. He went to Holland to secure money, immigrants, and teachers for the state schools. He secured half a million dollars with which to build a railroad from his seat of government to Delagoa Bay, and sent the railway material to Lourenzo Marques, where the rust is eating it to-day.

When Burgers returned to Pretoria, the capital of the republic, he found that Chief Secoceni, of the big Bapedi tribe, had defied the power of his Government, and was murdering the white immigrants in cold blood.

Burgers led his army in person to punish Secoceni, and captured one of the native strongholds, but was so badly defeated afterward that his soldiers became disheartened and decided to return to their homes.

Heavy war taxes were levied, and when the farmers were unable to pay them the Government was impotent to conduct its ordinary affairs, much less quell the rebellion of the natives. The Boers were divided among themselves on the subject of further procedure, and a civil war was imminent. The British Government, hearing of the condition of the republic's affairs, sent Sir Theophilus Shepstone, who had held a minor office at Natal, to Pretoria with almost limitless powers. He called upon President Burgers and stated to him that his mission was to annex the country to England, and gave as his reasons for such a proceeding the excuse that the unsettled condition of the native races demanded it.

Burgers pointed out to Shepstone that the native races had not harmed the English colonies, and that a new constitution, modelled after that of America, with a standing police force of two hundred mounted men, would put an end to all the republic's troubles with the natives. Shepstone, however, had the moral support of a small party of Boers who were dissatisfied with Burgers' administration, and on April 12, 1877, declared the republic a possession of the British Empire. Burgers retired from the presidency under protest, and Shepstone established a form of government that for a short time proved acceptable to many of the Boers. He renamed the country Transvaal, and added a considerable military force.

But the Boers were not accustomed to foreign interference in their affairs, and twice sent deputations to England to have the government of the country returned to their own hands. Paul Kruger was a member of both deputations, which showed ample proof that the annexation was made without the consent of the majority of the Boers, but the English Colonial Office refused to withdraw the British flag from the Transvaal.

Sir Owen Lanyon, a man of no tact and an inordinate hater of the Boers, succeeded

Shepstone as administrator of the Transvaal in 1879, and in a short time aroused the anger of his subjects to such an extent that an armed resistance to the British Government was decided upon. The open rebellion was delayed a short time by the election of Mr. Gladstone as Prime Minister of England, and, as he had publicly declared the righteousness of the Boer cause, the people of the Transvaal looked to him for their independence. When Mr. Gladstone refused to interfere in the Transvaal affairs the Boers held a meeting on the present site of Krugersdorp, and elected Paul Kruger, M. W. Pretorius, and Pieter J. Joubert a triumvirate to conduct the government.

At this meeting each Boer, holding a stone in his hand, took an oath before the Almighty that he would shed the last drop of blood, if need were, for his beloved country. The stones were cast into one great heap, over which a tall monument was erected several years afterward. The monument is annually made the rendezvous of large numbers of Boers, who there renew the solemn pledges to protect their country from aggressors.

On the national holiday, Dingaan's Day, December 16, 1880, the four-colour flag of the republic was again raised at the temporary capital at Heidelberg. The triumvirate sent a manifesto to Sir Owen Lanyon explaining the causes of discontent, and ending with this significant sentence, which has ever remained a motto of the individual Boers:

"We declare before God, who knows the heart, and before the world, that the people of the South African Republic have never been subjects of Her Majesty, and never will be."

Lanyon cursed the men who brought the manifesto to him, and straightway proceeded to execute the authority he possessed. His soldiers fired on a party of Boers proceeding toward Potchefstrom, where they intended to have the proclamation of independence printed. The Boers defeated the soldiers the same day the Transvaal flag was hoisted at Heidelberg, and the war, which had been impending for several months, was suddenly precipitated before either of the contestants was prepared.

Lanyon ordered the garrison of two hundred and sixty-four men at Leydenburg, under

THE EARLY HISTORY OF THE BOER RACE 57

Colonel Anstruther, to proceed to Pretoria, the English capital. At Bronkhorst Spruit, Colonel Anstruther's force was met by an equal number of Boers, who immediately attacked him. The engagement was brief but terrible, and the English forces were compelled to surrender.

Lanyon then sent to Natal for assistance, and Sir George Colley and a body of more than a thousand trained soldiers and volunteers set out to assist the English in the Transvaal, who for the most part were besieged in the different towns. Commandant-General Pieter Joubert, with a force of about fifteen hundred Boers, went forward into Natal for the purpose of meeting Colley, and occupied a narrow passage in the mountains known as Laing's Nek. Colley attempted to force the pass on January 28, 1881, but the Boers inflicted such a heavy loss upon his forces that he was compelled to retreat to Mount Prospect and await the arrival of fresh troops from England.

Eleven days after the battle of Laing's Nek, General Colley and three hundred men, while patrolling the road near the Ingogo River, were attacked by a body of Boers under Commandant Nicholaas Smit. The Boers killed and wounded two thirds of the English force engaged, and compelled the others to retreat in disorder. Up to this time the Boers had lost seventeen men killed and twenty-eight wounded, while the British loss was two hundred and fifty killed and three hundred and fifty wounded.

During the night of February 26th General Colley made a move which was responsible for one of the greatest displays of bravery the world has ever seen. The fight at Majuba Hill was won by the Boers against greater odds than have been encountered by any volunteer force in modern times, and is an example of the courage, bravery, and absolute confidence of the Boers when they believe they are divinely guided.

Between the camps of General Colley and Commandant-General Joubert lay Majuba Hill, a plateau with precipitous sides and a perfectly level top about twenty-five hundred feet above the camps. In point of resemblance

Majuba Hill, where one hundred and fifty Boer volunteers defeated six hundred British soldiers.

the hill was a huge inverted tub whose summit could only be reached by a narrow path. General Colley and six hundred men, almost all of whom were trained soldiers fresh from England, ascended the narrow path by moonlight, and when the sun rose in the morning were able to look from the summit of the hill and see the Boer camp in the valley.

The plan of campaign was that the regiments that had been left behind in camp should attempt to force the pass through Laing's Nek, and that the force on Majuba Hill should make a new attack on the Boers and in that manner crush the enemy in the pass. So positive were the soldiers of the success that awaited their plans that they looked down from their lofty position into the enemy's lines and speculated on the number of Boers that would live to tell the story of the battle.

It was Sunday morning, and had the distance between the two armies been less, the soldiers on the hill might have heard the sound of many voices singing hymns of praise and the prayers that were being offered by the Boers kneeling in the valley. The English held their enemies in the palm of their hand, it seemed, and with a few heavy guns they could have killed them by the score. The sides of the hill were so steep that it did not enter the minds of the English that the Boers would attempt to ascend except by the same path which they had traversed, and that was impossible, because the path leading from the base was occupied by the remaining English forces.

The idea that the Boers would climb from terrace to terrace, from one bush to another, and gain the summit in that manner, occurred to no one. Before there was any stir in the Boers' camp the English soldiers stood on the edge of the summit and, shaking their fists in exultation, challenged the enemy: "Come up here, you beggars!"

The Boers soon discovered the presence of the English on the hill, and the camp presented such an animated scene that the English soldiers were led to imagine that consternation had seized the Boers, and that they were preparing for a retreat.

THE EARLY HISTORY OF THE BOER RACE 61

A short time afterward, when the Boers marched toward the base of the hill, the illusion was dispelled; and still later, when one hundred and fifty volunteers from the Boer army commenced to ascend the sides of the hill, the former spirit of braggadocio which characterized the British soldier resolved itself into a feeling of nervousness. During the forenoon the British soldiers fired at such of the climbing Boers as they could see, but the Boers succeeded in dodging from one stone to another, so that only one of their number was killed in the ascent.

When the one hundred and fifty Boers reached the summit of the hill, after an arduous climb of more than five hours, they lay behind rocks at the edge and commenced a hot fire at the English soldiers, who had retreated into the centre of the plateau, thirty yards distant. The English soldiers had been ordered to fix their bayonets and were prepared to charge, but the order was never given. A fresh party of Boers had reached the summit and threatened to flank the English, who, having lost many of their officers and scores of men, became wildly panic-stricken.

Several minutes after General Colley was killed, the British soldiers who had escaped from the storm of bullets broke for the edge of the summit and allowed themselves to drop and roll down the sides of the hill. When the list of casualties was completed it was found that the Boers had killed ninety-two, wounded one hundred and thirty-four, and taken prisoners fifty-nine soldiers of the six hundred who ascended the hill. The loss on the Boers' side was one killed and five wounded.

A short time after the fight at Majuba Hill an armistice was arranged between Sir Evelyn Wood, the successor of General Colley, and the Triumvirate, and this led to the partial restoration of the independence of the South African Republic. By the terms of peace concluded between the two Governments, the suzerainty of Great Britain was imposed as one of the conditions, but this was afterward modified so that the Transvaal became absolutely independent in everything relating to its internal affairs. Great Britain, however, retained the right to veto treaties which the Transvaal Government might make with foreign countries.

CHAPTER III

THE JOHANNESBURG GOLD FIELDS

SOUTH AFRICA has many stories concerning the early history of the Witwatersrandt gold district, so that it is well-nigh impossible to discriminate between the fiction and the truth. One of the most probable stories has it that the former owner of the Randt region died recently in an almshouse in Surrey, England. He had a marvellous war record, having fought with the British army in the Crimea, at Sebastopol, in the Indian Mutiny, Zululand, and at Majuba Hill. With his savings of four thousand dollars he is said to have purchased fifteen thousand acres of land in the southern part of the Transvaal. He was obliged to forfeit his property to the Boer Government in 1882, because he had taken up arms against the Boers when they were fighting for their independence.

The actual discovery of gold in the Trans-

THE JOHANNESBURG GOLD FIELDS 65

vaal territory is credited to a German named Mauch, who travelled through that part of the country early in the century. He returned to Berlin with wonderful reports of the gold he had found, and attempted to enlist capital to work the mines. Whether his reports were not credited, or whether the Germans feared the natives, is not recorded, but Mauch is not heard of again in connection with the later history of the country. In 1854 a Dutchman named Jan Marais, who had a short time before returned from the Australian gold fields, prospected in the Transvaal, and found many evidences of gold. The Boers, fearing that their land would be overrun with gold-seekers, paid five hundred pounds to Marais, and sent him home after extracting a promise that he would not reveal his secret to any one.

It was not until 1884 that England heard of the presence of gold in South Africa. A man named Fred Stuben, who had spent several years in the country, spread such marvellous reports of the underground wealth of the Transvaal that only a short time elapsed before hundreds of prospectors and miners left

England for South Africa. When the first prospectors discovered auriferous veins of wonderful quality on a farm called Sterkfontein, the gold boom had its birth. It required the lapse of only a short time for the news to reach Europe, America, and Australia, and immediately thereafter that vast and widely scattered army of men and women which constantly awaits the announcement of new discoveries of gold was set in motion toward the Randt.

The Indian, Russian, American, and Australian gold fields were deserted, and the steamships and sailing vessels to South Africa were overladen with men and women of all degrees and nationalities. The journey to the Randt was expensive, dangerous, and comfortless, but before a year had passed almost twenty thousand persons had crossed the deserts and the plains and had settled on claims purchased from the Boers. In December, 1885, the first stamp mill was erected for the purpose of crushing the gneiss rock in which the gold lay hidden. This enterprise marks the real beginning of the gold fields of the Randt, which now yield one third of the world's total product of the precious metal. The advent of thousands of foreigners was a boon to the Boers, who owned the large farms on which the auriferous veins were located. Options on farms that were of little value a short time before were sold at incredible figures, and the prices paid for small claims would have purchased farms of thousands of acres two years before.

In July, 1886, the Government opened nine farms to the miners, and all have since become the best properties on the Randt. The names by which the farms were known were retained by the mines which were located upon them afterward, and, as they give an idea of the nomenclature of the country, are worth repetition : Langlaagte, Dreifontein, Rantjeslaagte, Doornfontein, Vogelstruitsfontein, Paardeplaats, Turffontein, Elandsfontein, and Roodepoort.

The railroad from Cape Town extended only as far north as the diamond mines at Kimberley, and the remainder of the distance, about five hundred miles, had to be traversed with ox-teams or on foot; but the gold-seekers yielded to no impediments, and marched in bodies of hundreds to the new fields. The machinery necessary to operate the mines and extract the gold from the rocks, as well as every ounce of food and every inch of lumber, was dragged overland by ox-teams, and the vast plains that had seen naught but the herds of Boer farmers and the wandering tribes of natives were quickly transformed into scenes of unparalleled activity.

On the Randt the California scenes of '49 were being re-enacted. Tents and houses of sheet iron were erected with picturesque lack of beauty and uniformity, and during the latter part of 1886 the community had reached such proportions that the Government marked off a township and called it Johannesburg. The Government, which owned the greater part of the land, held three sales of building lots, or "stands," as they are called in the Transvaal, and realized more than three hundred thousand dollars from the sales. The prices of stands measuring fifty by one hundred feet ranged from one dollar to one thousand dollars. Millions were secured in England and Europe for the development of the mines, and the individual miner sold his claims to companies with unlimited capital. The incredibly large dividends that were realized by some of the investors led to too heavy investments in the Stock Exchange in 1889, and a panic resulted. Investors lost thousands of pounds, and for several months the future of the gold fields appeared to be most gloomy. The opening of the railway to Johannesburg and the re-establishment of stock values caused a renewal of confidence, and the growth and development of the Randt was imbued with renewed vigour.

Owing to the Boers' lack of training and consequent inability to share in the development of the gold fields, the new industry remained almost entirely in the hands of the newcomers, the Uitlanders, and two totally different communities were created in the republic. The Uitlanders, who, in 1890, numbered about one hundred thousand, lived almost exclusively in Johannesburg and the suburbs along the Randt. The Boers, having disposed of their farms and lands on the Randt, were obliged to occupy the other parts of the republic, where they could follow their pastoral and agricultural pursuits.

The natural contempt which the Englishmen, who composed the majority of the Uitlander population, always have for persons and races not their intellectual or social equals, soon created a gulf between the Boers and the newcomers. This line of cleavage was extended when the newcomers attempted to obtain a foothold in the politics of the country. The Boers, who had been suddenly outnumbered three to one, naturally resented the interference, especially as it came from persons who had no desire to become permanent residents of the country, and who wanted a voice in the conduct of the national affairs only as a means to attain their own ends, without caring about the welfare of the entire republic.

The Uitlanders had many good and honest men among them, but the majority consisted of speculators, cutthroats, " I. D. B.," * and such others as were exiled from their native

---

* Illicit Diamond Buyers. Every diamond mined in the country must be registered with the Government, and may not be sold except by a licensed broker. Transgression of this law is called illicit diamond buying or selling, and is punishable with long imprisonment on the Breakwater at Cape Town.

lands by reason of crimes they had committed. Their cry was "Gold!" and honour and justice were cast to the winds. The Boer Government was blamed for famine, drought, and the locusts, and everything was done to embarrass those who were trying to administer justice to Boer and Uitlander alike.

One example is sufficient to show the conduct of the Uitlanders toward the Boers, but thousands could be given. President Kruger journeyed to Johannesburg in order to learn from the newcomers what his government might do to improve the industry. A crowd met Mr. Kruger, and, after rude remarks on his personal appearance, sang "God save the Queen." Later the Transvaal flag was torn down from a staff in front of the house in which the President was conferring with leading residents of the city. The Transvaal Government, on the other hand, sought by all means in its power to secure the good-will of the newcomers, and frequent conferences between leading men of the Randt and the officials of the Government were held with that object in view. The Second Volksraad was created, so that the Uitlanders might have a voice in the Government, and many reforms, which at the time were warmly approved by the Johannesburg Chamber of Mines, representing the mining population, were instituted, and would have been completed, satisfactory to all, had the Uitlanders waited, instead of plotting for the overthrow of the Government.

When the disturbing element of the Uitlander population found that their efforts to govern the Randt according to their own desires were fruitless, Cecil J. Rhodes, then Premier of Cape Colony and at the height of his influence, began his campaign for the control of the Boer territory. He brought to bear all the power at his command to harass the Pretorian Government, and tried in a score of ways to induce the colonial secretary to interfere in behalf of the Uitlanders, even going to the extent of offering to Secretary for the Colonies Chamberlain the payment of an equal share in the cost of a war with the Transvaal.

Whether Mr. Rhodes's real object in attempting to secure possession of the Transvaal was that he and other capitalists might consolidate the mines and limit the output, as he had done at Kimberley, or whether his earth-hunger impelled him, is known only to himself. Whatever the reason, he planned like a professional South American revolutionist, and by his boldness caused the amateur revolutionists of the Randt to gasp.

The opening prelude of the Jameson raid was a mass meeting held in November, 1895, by the Johannesburg Chamber of Mines, which had always shown marked friendliness to the Pretorian Government. The president of the organization, Lionel Phillips, created a sensation by reading a mass of alleged grievances against the Government, as formulated by an organization called the "Transvaal National Union," and threatening that, unless the Government gave immediate remedy, revolutionary methods would be adopted in order to obtain redress. The plot had begun its evolution, and its success was to be attained in a certain well-defined way.

The speech of Mr. Phillips was to serve as Johannesburg's ultimatum to the Boers. If the Government gave no heed, the revolutionary party was to seize Johannesburg by force of arms, declare a provisional government of the country, and march against Pretoria. Once in possession of the seat of government, it was planned to lay their grievances before the world, and ask that the future government of the country be placed in the hands of the majority of the white population. It was believed that if the plans were thoroughly perfected the plot could be carried to a successful conclusion without the firing of a single shot. In order to be amply prepared in case the Boers should make an unexpected resistance to the revolutionists, it had been arranged with Dr. Leander Starr Jameson, who was then in charge of the troops of Mr. Rhodes's British South Africa Company, to ride across the border to Johannesburg, a journey of several days, and assist in the engagement. The revolution was perfectly planned, and it would have required only half an effort on the part of a Haytien revolutionist to carry it out successfully; but Mr. Rhodes, the brains of the movement, was in Cape Town, and unable to do anything more practical than imagine that his plans were being followed. By common agreement among the revolutionists, Dr. Jameson and Mr. Rhodes, it was decided to have the uprising in Johannesburg about the 28th of December, and everything had been planned accordingly. From Kimberley Mr. Rhodes's De Beers Company had sent two thousand rifles—the Boers say twenty thousand—one hundred and twenty-five cases of ammunition, and three Maxims in oil casks across the border into Johannesburg, where the Uitlanders were secretly organizing and drilling military companies. In the British territory Dr. Jameson and his six hundred troopers were polishing their rifles and Maxims, and waiting for the day when they should march toward Johannesburg.

Under pretence that they were to be used in connection with a new stage line to be opened, "canteens," or feeding places, had been established several miles apart on the road over which the troopers were supposed to enter Johannesburg, and all had been bountifully stocked with provisions for soldier and horse. The Government at Pretoria had been led to believe that Johannesburg was armed to the teeth, and that nothing could prevent the dissolution of the republic.

When the 28th day of December arrived, the well-advertised revolution had not materialized, and nothing more martial was to be seen than several regiments of civilians drilling in the streets. Thousands of men, women, and children, fearing that the Boers might attack the city at any moment, besieged the railway station, and fought like so many uncivilized beings to board the trains leaving for Natal and Cape Colony. Among those who displayed the greatest eagerness to escape from the city were many wealthy Englishmen, who several days before had been the most rabid sympathizers of the revolutionary movement. The city was in the hands of the Uitlanders, because the handful of Transvaal police, commonly called "Zarps," had been withdrawn by the Boer authorities, who depended on the power of the guns in the fort on the outskirts of the town to quell any disturbance that might be made. There was no actual revolution, because the Uitlanders were divided among

THE JOHANNESBURG GOLD FIELDS 77

themselves as to the course to be pursued. The Englishmen, as soon as the success of the movement seemed so close at hand, aroused the enmity of the other Uitlanders by asking them to consent to the raising of the British flag as soon as the Boer Republic had been obliterated. This campaign placed the revolution in an entirely different light to those of the Uitlanders who had no particular liking for England, and the result was that the revolutionary party was divided into two camps. On the side of the Englishmen were the Uitlanders from British colonies—Scotchmen, Irishmen, Welshmen, Canadians, Australians, and all the Americans who were employed by British mines. In the other camp were the Germans, Frenchmen, Scandinavians, Swedes, Norwegians, Danes, and Finlanders.

The majority of the Americans felt that a revolution was unjustifiable, although some of the grievances complained of were undoubtedly just, and ranged themselves on the anti-English side. Another reason for the Americans' attitude at that time was President Cleveland's warlike message to England on the Venezuelan boundary dispute. The real American patriot is found ten thousand miles from home, and those in America who were excited when they heard of England's attempt to grasp a swamp in far-away Venezuela can readily imagine the spirit of the Americans in the Transvaal who saw England attempting to steal a valuable country without the shadow of an excuse.

The following day, the 29th of December, Dr. Jameson and his troopers, believing that the revolutionists at Johannesburg had seized the city, as it had been planned they should do, crossed the border into the Transvaal. Messages had been sent to Mr. Rhodes and others of the leaders, stating the time of the departure from British territory and the time set for their arrival in Johannesburg. Several troopers were sent ahead to cut the telegraph wires, so that no news of the expedition should reach the outside world; but the anticipated joy of reaching Johannesburg and assisting in raising the "Union Jack." intoxicated the men, and they succeeded in cutting only the wire which led to Cape Town. The wire to Pretoria remained

THE JOHANNESBURG GOLD FIELDS

untouched, and before the troopers had proceeded fifty miles into Transvaal territory the Pretorian Government was aware of their approach, and made preparations to meet them.

The Uitlanders in Johannesburg had been led to believe by their *dilettante* leaders that Dr. Jameson's incursion had been postponed, and they were ignorant of his whereabouts until the following day, when a member of the Pretorian Government kind-heartedly gave the information to several of the Uitlander leaders, who had journeyed to Pretoria with rifles in one hand and demands in the other. When the news of the invasion reached Johannesburg the excitement became intensified. A reform committee of about one hundred persons was quickly formed, and into their hands was given the conduct of the revolution. Speeches were made from the balcony of the Stock Exchange, until some practical speaker suggested that it would be proper to unpack the rifles and ammunition from the oil casks if the revolution was to be undertaken.

The suggestion was acted upon, and late that night five hundred of the rifles to be used in the overthrow of a republic were being carried to and fro in the streets of Johannesburg on the shoulders of men who were willing to do the work for ten dollars a night. The following day, while Dr. Jameson and his troopers were marching over the veldt toward Johannesburg, the leaders of the movement made more speeches to the crowd at the Stock Exchange, and waited for news from Pretoria instead of making news for Pretoria.

The first part of the plot—the capture of Johannesburg—had been successful without the discharge of a rifle, because the Boers had withdrawn their police, and there remained no one at which the *opéra-bouffe* revolutionists might fire.

The next step was the capture of Pretoria, and for this purpose a small expedition started for the capital city; but returned hastily and without their rifles and ammunition when they saw a thousand Boers, each with the usual accompaniment of a rifle, attending the annual "Nachtmaal," or communion, in the city.

The last day of the year saw the Uitlanders undecided as to what action to take. On the one hand was Dr. Jameson coming to their relief, while on the other was the Pretorian Government preparing to quell an insurrection which had not even started. The Reform Committee, whose members a few weeks before had made arrangements for Dr. Jameson's coming, denied that they had any connection with the invasion. Dr. Jameson having been repudiated, the committee debated for many hours on the subject of which flag should be hoisted in the event that the revolution was successful, and finally sent John Hays Hammond, an American member of the committee, to secure the four-colour of the Transvaal.

Then and there the most ludicrous incident of the Uitlander rising took place. With uplifted hands the members of the committee, who were the leaders of the revolution, swore allegiance to the red, white, green, and blue flag of the Transvaal, which for days and months before they had reviled and insulted. After having vowed loyalty to the Transvaal flag, the committee continued the preparations for the defence of the city and the drilling of the volunteers who were enrolled at a score of different shops in the city. A rumour that Dr. Jameson had been attacked by the Boer forces, but had repulsed them, gave additional zest to the military preparations, and the advisability of sending some of the mounted troops to meet him was discussed but not acted upon. The reported victory of Dr. Jameson's troopers, coupled with a request from the Pretorian Government for a conference to discuss methods of ending the troubles, caused the Reform Committee to repent their hasty action in swearing allegiance to the Transvaal flag, and they were on the point of breaking their obligation, and sending aid to the invading troopers, when, during the last hour of the year, they learned that the secretary for the colonies, Mr. Chamberlain, had repudiated and recalled Dr. Jameson.

The first day of the new year the spirit of the Uitlanders was dampened by the information that the Boers were massing troops on the outskirts of the town; and, fearing that the town might be attacked at any moment, the Reform Committee, which had been spending

THE JOHANNESBURG GOLD FIELDS 83

much energy in informing the Pretorian Government of the city's great military preparation, telegraphed pathetic appeals for assistance to the British High Commissioner at Cape Town. Couriers arrived from the outskirts of the city and reported that Dr. Jameson and his troopers were within fifteen miles of Johannesburg, and plans were made to receive him. One small regiment left the city to meet the troopers and escort them into the city, while the remainder of the revolutionary forces held jubilation festivities in honour of Dr. Jameson's anticipated arrival.

While Johannesburg, which had promised to do the fighting, was in the midst of its festival joys, Dr. Jameson and those of his six hundred troopers who were not dead on the fields of battle were waving a Hottentot woman's white apron in token of their surrender to the Boer forces at Doornkop, eighteen miles away. The Johannesburg revolt, initiated by magnificent promises, ended with an inglorious display of that quality which the British have been wont to attribute to Boers—"funk." The British have their Balaclava and Sebastopol, but they also have their Majuba Hill and the Johannesburg revolt.

The final scenes of the Jameson raid, which might more fittingly be called "the Johannesburg funk," were enacted in Pretoria, where Dr. Jameson and the other prisoners were taken, and in London, where the officers of the expedition were tried and virtually acquitted. The revolutionists in Johannesburg yielded all their arms and ammunition to the Boer Government, which in turn made every possible effort to effect an amicable settlement of the grievances of the Uitlanders. But the raid left a deeper impress upon Johannesburg and its interests than any of its organizers or supporters had ever dreamed of. Almost one fifth of the inhabitants of the city left the country for more peaceable localities in the three months following the disturbance, and business became stagnant. Capitalists declined to invest more money in the gold mines while the unsettled condition of the political affairs continued, and scores of mines were compelled to abandon operations. Stocks fell in value, and thousands of pounds were lost by innocent shareholders in Europe, who were ignorant of the political affairs of the country. For two years the depression continued, and so acute were its results that hundreds of respectable miners and business men, who had been accustomed to live in luxury, became bankrupt, and were obliged to beg for their food. Those who were able to do so sold their interests in the city and left the country, while hundreds of others would have been happy to leave had they been able to secure passage to their native countries.

During the last year the effects of the raid have been disappearing and the commercial interests of the Randt have been improving, but the political atmosphere has been kept vibrating at a continuous loss to the industries that are represented in the country. All South Africa was similarly affected by the depression, which naturally cut off the revenue from the gold fields and that derived from passengers and freight coming into the country from foreign shores. To add to the general dismay, the entire country was scourged with the rinderpest, a disease which killed more than a million and a half cattle; clouds of locusts, that destroyed all vegetation and made life miserable; and a long drought.

After the scourges had passed, and the political atmosphere had become somewhat clarified, the industries of Johannesburg and the Randt returned to their normal condition, and the development of the natural resources of the territory was resumed. Many of those persons who deserted the city during its period of depression returned with renewed energy, and those who had successfully combated the storm joined with the newcomers in welcoming the return of prosperous times. Confidence was restored among the European capitalists, and money was again freely invested and trade relations firmly re-established.

Johannesburg after the Jameson raid was a distressing scene; the Johannesburg of to-day is a wondrous testimonial to the energy and progress of mankind.

If there were no other remarkable features to mark the last decade of the twentieth century, the marvellous city which has been built near the heart of the Dark Continent would alone be a fitting monument to the enterprise and achievements of the white race during that period of time.

CHAPTER IV

THE BOER OF TO-DAY

THE wholesale slander and misrepresentation with which the Boers of South Africa have been pursued can not be outlived by them in a hundred years. It originated when the British forces took possession of the Cape of Good Hope, and it has continued with unabated vigour ever since. Recently the chief writers of fiction have been prominent Englishmen, who, on hunting expeditions or rapid tours through the country, saw the object of their venom from car windows or in the less favourable environments of a trackless veldt.

In earlier days the outside world gleaned its knowledge of the Boers from certain British statesmen, who, by grace of Downing Street, controlled the country's colonial policy, and consequently felt obliged to conjure up weird descriptions of their far-distant subjects in order to make the application of certain harsh policies appear more applicable and necessary. Missionaries to South Africa, traders, and, not least of all, speculators, all found it convenient to traduce the Boers to the people in England, and the object in almost every case was the attainment of some personal end. Had there been any variety in the complaints, there might have been reason to suppose they were justifiable, but the similarity of the reports led to the conclusion that the British in South Africa were conducting the campaign of misrepresentation for the single purpose of arousing the enmity of the home people against the Boers. The unbiased reports were generally of such a nature that they were drowned by the roar of the malicious ones, and, instead of creating a better popular opinion of the race, only assisted in stirring the opposition to greater flights of fancy.

American interests in South Africa having been so infinitesimal until the last decade, our own knowledge of the country and its people naturally was of the same proportions. When Americans learned anything concerning South

Africa or the Boers it came by way of London, which had vaster interests in the country, and should have been able to give exact information. But, like other colonial information, it was discoloured with London additions, and the result was that American views of the Boers tallied with those of the Englishman.

Among the more prominent Englishmen who have recently studied the Boers from a car window, and have given the world the benefit of their opinions, is a man who has declared that the Boer blocked the way in South Africa, and must go. Among other declarations with which this usually well-informed writer has taken up the cudgel in behalf of his friend Mr. Rhodes, he has called the Boers " utterly detestable," " guilty of indecencies and family immorality," and even so " benighted and uncivilized " as to preclude the possibility of writing about them. All this he is reported to have said about a race that has been lauded beyond measure by the editors of every country in the world except those under the English flag. The real cause of it all is found in the Boers' disposition to carry their own burdens, and their disinclination to allow England to be their keeper. Their opinions of justice and right were formed years ago in Cape Colony, and so long as their fighting ability has not been proved in a negative manner, so long will the Boers be reviled by the covetous Englishmen of South Africa and their friends.

The Boer of to-day is a man who loves solitude above all things. He and his ancestors have enjoyed that chief product of South Africa for so many generations that it is his greatest delight to be alone. The nomadic spirit of the early settler courses in his veins, and will not be eradicated though cities be built up all around him and railroads hem him in on all sides.

He loves to be out on the veldt, where nothing but the tall grass obstructs his view of the horizon, and his happiness is complete when, gun in hand, he can stalk the buck or raise the covey on soil never upturned by the share of a plough. The real Boer is a real son of the soil. It is his natural environment, and he chafes when he is compelled to go where there are more than a dozen dwellings in the same square mile of area.

The pastoral life he and his ancestors have been leading has endowed him with a happy-go-lucky disposition. Some call him lazy and sluggish because he has plenty of time at his disposal and "counts ten" before acting. Others might call that disposition a realization of his necessities, and his chosen method of providing for them.

The watching of herds of cattle and flocks of sheep has since biblical times been considered an easier business than the digging of minerals or the manufacture of iron, and the Boer has realized that many years ago. He has also realized the utter uselessness of digging for minerals and the manufacture of iron when the products of either were valueless at a distance of a thousand miles from the nearest market. Taking these facts in consideration, the Boer has done what other less nomadic people have done. He has improved the opportunities which lay before him, and has allowed the others to pass untouched.

The Boers are not an agricultural people, because the nature of the country affords no encouragement for the following of that pursuit. The great heat of the summer removes rivers in a week and leaves rivulets hardly big enough to quench the thirst of the cattle. Irrigation is out of the question, as the great rivers are too far distant and the country too level to warrant the building of artificial waterways. Taking all things into consideration, there is nothing for a Boer to do but raise cattle and sheep, and he may regard himself particularly fortunate at the end of each year if drought and disease have not carried away one half of this wealth.

The Boer's habits and mode of life are similar to those of the American ranchman, and in reality there is not much difference between the two except that the latter is not so far removed from civilization. The Boer likes to be out of the sight of the smoke of his neighbour's house, and to live fifteen or twenty miles from another dwelling is a matter of satisfaction rather than regret to him. The patriarchal custom of the people provides against the lack of companionship which naturally would follow this custom.

When a Boer's children marry they settle within a short distance of the original family homestead; generally several hundred yards distant. In this way, in a few years, a small village is formed on the family estates, which may consist of from five hundred to ten thousand acres of uninclosed grazing ground. Every son when he marries is entitled to a share of the estate, which he is supposed to use for the support of himself and his family, and in that way the various estates grow smaller each generation. When an estate grows too small to support the owner, he "treks" to another part of the country, and receives from the state such an amount of territory as he may require.

Boer houses, as a rule, are situated a long distance away from the tracks of the transport wagons, in order that passing infected animals may not introduce disease into the flocks and herds of the farmer. Strangers are seldom seen as a result of this isolation, and news from the outer world does not reach the Boers unless

THE BOER OF TO-DAY

they travel to the towns to make the annual purchases of necessaries.

Their chief recreation is the shooting of game, which abounds in almost all parts of the country. Besides being their recreation, it is also their duty, for it is much cheaper to kill a buck and use it to supply the family larder than to kill an ox or a sheep for the same purpose. It is seldom that a Boer misses his aim, be the target a deer or an Englishman, and he has ample time to become proficient in the use of the rifle. His gun is his constant companion on the veldt and at his home, and the long alliance has resulted in earning for him the distinction of being the best marksman and the best irregular soldier in the world. The Boer is not a sportsman in the American sense of the word. He is a hunter, pure and simple, and finds no delight in following the Englishman's example of spending many weeks in the Zambezi forests or the dangerous Kalahari Desert, and returning with a giraffe tail and a few horns and feathers as trophies of the chase. He hunts because he needs meat for his family and leather for sjam-bok whips with which to drive his cattle, and not because it gives him personal gratification to be able to demonstrate his supreme skill in the tracking of game.

The dress of the Boer is of the roughest description and material, and suited to his occupation. Corduroy and flannel for the body, a wide-brimmed felt hat for the head, and soft leather-soled boots fitted for walking on the grass, complete the regulation Boer costume, which is picturesque as well as serviceable. The clothing, which is generally made by the Boer's vrouw, or wife, makes no pretension of fit or style, and is quite satisfactory to the wearer if it clings to the body. In most instances it is built on plans made and approved by the Voortrekkers of 1835, and quite satisfactory to the present Boers, their sons, and grandsons.

Physically, the Boers are the equals, if not the superiors, of their old-time enemy, the Zulus. It would be difficult to find anywhere an entire race of such physical giants as the Boers of the Transvaal and the Orange Free State. The roving existence, the life in the open air, and the freedom from disturbing cares have combined to make of the Boers a race that is almost physically perfect. If an average height of all the full-grown males in the country were taken, it would be found to be not less than six feet two inches, and probably more. Their physique, notwithstanding their comparatively idle mode of living, is magnificently developed.

The action of the almost abnormally developed muscles of the legs and arms, discernible through their closely fitting garments, gives an idea of the remarkable powers of endurance which the Boers have displayed on many occasions when engaged in native and other campaigns. They can withstand almost any amount of physical pain and discomfort, and can live for a remarkably long time on the smallest quantity of food. It is a matter of common knowledge that a Boer can subsist on a five-pound slice of "biltong"—beef that has been dried in the sun until it is almost as hard as stone—for from ten to fifteen days without suffering any pangs of hunger. In times of war, "biltong" is the principal item in the army rations, and in peace, when he is following his flocks, it also is the Boer shepherd's chief article of diet.

The religion of the Boers is one of their greatest characteristics, and one that can hardly be understood when it is taken into consideration that they have been separated for almost two hundred years from the refining influences of a higher civilization. The simple faith in a Supreme Being, which the original emigrants from Europe carried to South Africa, has been handed down from one generation to another, and in two centuries of fighting, trekking, and ranching has lost none of its pristine depth and fervour.

With the Boer his religion is his first and uppermost thought. The Old Testament is the pattern which he strives to follow. The father of the family reads from its pages every day, and from it he formulates his ideas of right and wrong as they are to be applied to the work of the day. Whether he wishes to exchange cattle with his neighbour or give his daughter in marriage to a neighbour's son, he consults the Testament, and finds therein the advice that is applicable to the situation. He

Kirk Street, Pretoria, with the State Church in the distance.

reads nothing but the Bible, and consequently his belief in its teachings is indestructible and supreme.

His religious temperament is portrayed in almost every sentence he utters, and his repetition of biblical parables and sayings is a custom which so impresses itself upon the mind of the stranger that it is but natural that those who are unacquainted with the Boer should declare it a sure sign of his hypocrisy. He does not quote Scripture merely to impress upon the mind of his hearer the fact that he is a devout Christian, but does it for the same reasons that a sailor speaks the language of the seafarer.

The Boer is a low churchman among low churchmen. He abhors anything that has the slightest tendency toward show or outward signs of display in religious worship. He is simple in his other habits, and in his religious observances he is almost primitively simple. To him the wearing of gorgeous raiment, special attitudes, musical accompaniment to hymns, and special demonstrations are the rankest sacrilege. Of the nine legal holidays in the Transvaal, five—Good Friday, Easter Monday, Ascension Day, Whit Monday, and Christmas—are Church festival days, and are strictly observed by every Boer in the country.

The Dutch Reformed Church has been the state Church since 1835, when the Boers commenced emigrating from Cape Colony. The "trekkers" had no regularly ordained ministers, but depended upon the elders for their religious training, as well as for leadership in all temporal affairs. One of the first clergymen to preach to the Boers was an American, the Rev. Daniel Lindley, who was one of the earliest missionaries ever sent to South Africa. The state controls the Church, and, conversely, the Church controls the state, for it is necessary for a man to become a factor in religious affairs before he can become of any political importance. As a result of this custom, the politicians are necessarily the most active church members.

The Hervormde Dopper branch of the Dutch Reformed Church is the result of a disagreement in 1883 with the Gereformeerde branch over the singing of hymns during a religious service. The Doppers, led by Paul Kruger, peaceably withdrew, and started a congregation of their own when the more progressive faction insisted on singing hymns, which the Doppers declared was extremely worldly.

Since then the two chief political parties are practically based on the differences in religion. The Progressive party is composed of those who sing hymns, and the members of the Conservative party are those who are more Calvinistic in their tendencies. As the Conservatives have been in power for the last decade, it follows that the majority of the Boers are opposed to the singing of hymns in church. The greatest festival in the Boer calendar is that of Nachtmaal, or Communion, which is generally held in Pretoria the latter part of the year.

The majority of the Boers living in remote parts of the country, where established congregations or churches are an impossibility, it behooves every Boer to journey to the capital once a year to partake of communion. Pretoria then becomes the Mecca of all Boers, and the pretty little town is filled to overflowing with pilgrims and their "trekking" wagons and cattle. Those who live in remote parts of the country are obliged to start several weeks before the Nachtmaal in order to be there at the appointed time, and the whole journey to and fro in many instances requires six weeks' time. When they reach Pretoria they bivouac in the open square surrounding the old brick church in the centre of the town, and spend almost all their time in the church. It is one of the grandest scenes in South Africa to observe the pilgrims camping in the open square under the shade of the patriarchal church, which to them is the most sacred edifice in the world.

The home life of the Boers is as distinctive a feature of these rough, simple peoples as is their deep religious enthusiasm. If there is anything that his falsifiers have attacked, it is the Boer's home life, and those who have had the opportunity to study it will vouch that none more admirable exists anywhere. The Boer heart is filled with an intense feeling of family affection. He loves his wife and children above all things, and he is never too busy to eulogize them. He will allow his flocks to wander a mile away while he relates a trifling incident of family life, and he would rather miss an hour's sleep than not take advantage of an opportunity to talk on domestic topics.

He does not gossip, because he sees his neighbours too rarely for that, but he will lay before you the detailed history and distinctive features of every one of his ancestors, relations, and descendants. He is hospitable to a degree that is astonishing, and he will give to a stranger the best room in the house, the use of his best horse, and his finest food. Naturally he will not give an effusive welcome to an Englishman, because he is the natural enemy of the Boer, but to strangers of other nationalities he opens his heart and house.

The programme of the Boer's day is hardly ever marred by any changes. He rises with the sun, and works among the sheep and cattle until breakfast. There at the table he meets his family and conducts the family worship. If the parents of the married couple are present, they receive the best seats at the table, and are treated with great reverence.

After breakfast he makes his plans for the day's work, which may consist of a forward " trek " or a hunting trip. He attends to the little plot of cultivated ground, which provides all the vegetables and grain for the table, and spends the remainder of the day in attending to the cattle and sheep. Toward night he gathers his family around him, and reads to them selected chapters from the Bible. From the same book he teaches his children to read until twilight is ended, whereupon the Boer's day is ended, and he seeks his bed.

During the dry season the programme varies only as far as his place of abode is concerned. With the arrival of that season the Boer closes his house and becomes a wanderer in pursuit of water. The sheep and cattle are driven to the rivers, and the family follows in big transport wagons, not unlike the American prairie-schooner, propelled by eight spans of oxen. The family moves from place to place as the necessity for new pasturage arises. With the approach of the wet season the nomads prepare for the return to the deserted homestead, and, as soon as the first rain has fallen and the grass has changed the colour of the landscape, the Boer and his vast herds are homeward bound.

The Boer homestead is as unpretentious as its owner. Generally it is a low, one-story stone structure, with a steep tile roof and a small annex in the rear, which is used as a kitchen. The door is on a level with the ground, and four windows afford all the light that is required in the four square rooms in the interior. A dining room and three bedrooms suffice for a family, however large. The floors are of hardened clay, liberally coated with manure, which is designed to ward off the pestiferous insects that swarm over the plains.

The house is usually situated in a valley and close to a stream, and, in rare instances, is sheltered by a few trees that have been brought from the coast country. Native trees are such a rarity that the traveller may go five hundred miles without seeing a single specimen. The Boer vrouw feels no need of firewood, however, for her ancestors taught her to cook her meals over a fire of the dry product of the cattle-decked plains.

Personal uncleanliness is one of the great failings that has been attributed to the Boer, but when it is taken into consideration that water is a priceless possession on the plains of South Africa, no further explanation is needed. The canard that the Boers go to bed without undressing is as absurd as the one of like origin that an entire family sleeps in one bed. Yet these fictions constantly appear, and frequently over the names of persons who have penetrated into South Africa no farther than Cape Town.

The Boer here depicted is the representative Boer—the one who shoulders his rifle and fights for his country; the one who watches his cattle on the plains and pays his taxes; the one who tries to improve his condition, and takes advantage of every opportunity for advancement that is offered. There is a worthless Boer, as there is a worthless Englishman, a worthless German, and a worthless American, but he is so far in the minority that he need not be analyzed.

There is, however, a Boer who lives in the towns and cities, and he compares favourably with other men of South African birth. He has had the advantage of better schools, and can speak one or more languages besides his own. He is not so nomadic in his tendencies as his rural countryman, and he has absorbed more of the modernisms. He can conduct a philosophic argument, and his wife and daughters can play the piano. If he is wealthy, his son is a student at a European university and his daughter flirting on the beach at Durban or attending a ladies' seminary at Bloemfontein or Grahamstown.

He is as progressive as any white man cares to be under that generous South African sun, and when it comes to driving a bargain he is a match for any of the money sharks of Johannesburg. For the youthful Boer who reaches the city directly from the country, without any trade or profession, the prospects are gloomy. He is at a great disadvantage when put into competition with almost any class of residents. The occupations to which he can turn are few, and these have been still further restricted in late years by the destruction of cattle by the rinderpest and the substitution of railways for road transport. His lack of education unfits him for most of the openings provided in such a city as Johannesburg, even when business is at its highest tide, and a small increase in the tension of business brings him to absolute want.

The Boer of to-day is a creature of circumstance. He is outstripped because he has had no opportunities for development. Driven from Cape Colony, where he was rapidly developing a national character, he was compelled to wander into lands that offered no opportunities of any description. He has been cut off for almost a hundred years from an older and more energetic civilization, and even from his neighbours; it is no wonder that he is a century behind the van. No other civilized race on earth has been handicapped in such a manner, and if there had been one it is a matter for conjecture whether it would have held its own, as the Boer has done, or whether it would have fallen to the level of the savage.

Had the Boer Voortrekkers been fortunate

enough to settle in a fertile country bordering on the sea, where they might have had communication with the outer world, their descendants would undoubtedly to-day be growing cane and wheat instead of herding cattle and driving transport wagons. Their love of freedom could not have been greater under those circumstances, but they might have averted the conditions which now threaten to erase their nation from the face of the earth.

CHAPTER V

PRESIDENT KRUGER

STEPHANUS JOHANNES PAULUS KRUGER, or Uncle Paul, the Lion of Rustenberg, is a man of most remarkable characteristics. A man of absolutely no education, as we understand the word, he has, during the long years of a notable career, so applied his inherent abilities, his natural astuteness, the cunning acquired by constant battling with the wiles of native enemies, as to be able to acquit himself of his high office in a manner to be envied by many who have enjoyed a hundred times as many advantages. Although he is almost seventy-five years old, the President's mind has not become dimmed, but, if anything, has grown keener of perception and wider in its scope during the last ten years.

Since his youth Mr. Kruger has been a leader among his countrymen. When a boy he had pronounced ability as a deer-stalker, and it is related of him that before he had reached manhood he had killed more lions than any other man in the colony. He was absolutely fearless, and could endure any amount of bodily pain and discomfort. As an example of this, I repeat his explanation of the accident that caused him to lose his left thumb:

"We were shooting rhinoceros one day," said he, "when an old gun exploded in my hands. It cut my thumb so badly that I saw it could not be saved. I borrowed a dull knife and cut the thumb off, because it prevented me from holding the gun properly."

President Kruger's personality is most unique. He impresses one as being a king in the garb of a farmer, a genius in a dunce's cap. At first sight he would be mistaken for an awkward countryman, with "store clothes" and a silk hat intended for some one else. His frock coat is far too small to reach around his corpulent body, and his trousers seem to have a natural antipathy for his shoes.

He wears no cuffs, and the presence of a collar and tie may be determined only by drawing aside the natural curtain formed by his whiskers. He is uncouth in his manner, but he has great natural attractiveness gained by a long life among hunters in the wilds. He is suspicious of everything and every one, but that quality is easily accounted for by his early dealings with negro chiefs, whose treacherous habits caused him to become wary in all his transactions with them. In later days this has stood him in good stead. He is slow to make friends, but once he trusts a person voluminous proof is necessary before he alters his opinion of the man. He never forgets a good deed, and never pardons the man who does a bad one.

President Kruger is short in stature, measuring less than five feet seven inches. His head and body are large and fat, but his legs are thin and short. His head is just a trifle longer than broad, and almost fits the English definition of "square head." The small eyes are surmounted by bushy, white eyebrows, which extend half an inch beyond his forehead.

When he is not sitting for a photograph his hair is not so neatly arranged as it appears in the well-known pictures, but hangs loosely down over his wide forehead, except when, with a hasty swish of the hand, he brushes it aside. The hair is nearly white, and hangs over the sides of his head in long tresses, which cover both his ears.

When he smiles the big fat circles above his cheeks are pushed upward, and shut his small gray eyes from view. But when pleased the President generally laughs hilariously, and then his eyes remain closed for the greater part of a minute. Mr. Kruger's nose and mouth are the chief features of his face. Both are more extensive than his large face demands, but they are such marvels in their own peculiar way as to be distinguishing marks. The bridge of the nose grows wide as it goes outward from the point between the eyes, and before it reaches the tip it has a gentle upheaval. Then it spreads out on either side, and covers fully two inches of area above his upper lip. It is not attractive, but in that it follows the general condition of his facial landscape.

The mouth is wide and ungainly. The constant use of a heavy pipe has caused a deep depression on the left side of his lower lip, and this gives the whole mouth the appearance of being unbalanced. His chin is large and prominent, and his ears correspond relatively in size and symmetry with his face. When in repose his features are not pleasant to look upon, but when lighted up by a smile they become rather attractive, and generally cause his laughter to become contagious among his hearers.

The thin line of beard which runs from ear to ear combines with the hair on his head in forming what is not unlike a white halo around the President's face. The lines in the man's face are deep, irregular, and very numerous. They indicate more than anything the ceaseless worry and troubles to which the President has been subjected while directing the affairs of his countrymen of the Transvaal.

The physical description of the Kruger of to-day is one that suggests sluggishness and idleness rather than alertness and ceaseless activity. The appearance of the man certainly does not conform with his record of marvellous performances, unflagging endeavour, and superior mental attainments. The well-preserved Kruger at seventy-five years bears no deep marks of the busy and eventful life he has led, nor are there any visible indications that the end of his usefulness to his people is close at hand.

The fragmentary history of Mr. Kruger's life, as related by himself, gives an insight into his remarkably varied experiences. He modestly refrains from allowing any one, even those who know him best, to obtain from him enough of his own history to incorporate in a biography, and it is likely, unless in his later years he changes his mind, that no detailed narrative can ever be written.

Although the majority of his countrymen are of Dutch or Huguenot ancestry, Mr. Kruger is of German descent. Jacob Kruger, his paternal ancestor, emigrated to South Africa, in 1713, from the Potsdam district of Germany, and married a young woman who was born in Cape Colony. He was born October 10, 1825, in Colesburg, Cape Colony, whither his parents had "trekked" from Cape Town a quarter of a century before. The first Krugers whose names appear in the Dutch East India Company's records arrived in the settlement at the Cape in 1712, and thereafter became leaders in enterprise among the settlers. While Mr. Kruger was yet in his infancy the Boers' troubles with the Colonial Government began, and when he was ten years old he migrated with the "Voortrekkers" to the unknown regions in the interior.

The life in the open and the tropical temperature served to develop him early, and at the age of fifteen we find him shooting his first lion, as well as serving in the capacity of "field cornet," a minor official position. As such he took part in the wars with the Zulu Dingaan and the Matabele Moselekatse, and served with distinction. In 1842 he was confirmed by the Rev. Daniel Lindley, the American missionary, and had implanted more firmly in his heart the religious feeling which in later years has proved to be his greatest solace in his troubles.

Next we hear of him standing by the side of his father while he fires the first shot at the English soldiers in the battle of Boomplaats, in 1848. After doing valiant service in that battle, he became one of the leaders of the "trekkers" who settled in the Transvaal country.

In 1856 young Kruger, then barely thirty-one years old, is elected sub-commandant of the Transvaal army, a most responsible position in a country where natives are as treacherous as they are innumerable. Five years later he becomes commandant of the army, and leads a force of one hundred and fifty men against Chief Sechele. He retains that office until 1877, when England annexes the country to her domain. During the war for independence which then ensues, Mr. Kruger is Vice-President of the Triumvirate, which executes the government of the country, and after peace is declared in 1883 he is elected to the presidency. He is thrice re-elected, and is now serving his fourth term as head of the South African Republic.

Into this skeleton of his life's story might be fitted innumerable incidents and anecdotes that are related by his countrymen, who treasure them greatly and repeat them at every opportunity. Many of these are probably imaginary, while others have undoubtedly been retold so frequently that they have lost all resemblance of the original form. The majority of the stories refer to Mr. Kruger's prowess in dealing with lions, tigers, and elephants, and many of these are probably true. Several of those that he himself verifies are given merely to illustrate the experiences that the Boers encountered in the early days of the "trekkers."

When fifteen years old Kruger and one of his sisters, being left alone on the veldt by their parents, were approached by a South African panther, small but of ample enough proportions to frighten the two children. Kruger, with only a knife for a weapon, boldly attacked the panther, and after a severe struggle, during which he was sorely injured, slew the beast. Another story, illustrative of his physical strength, is that he contested with a native in a foot-race of twelve hours' duration, and won by such a large margin that he was enabled to stalk a buck on the veldt and carry it to his father's house before his competitor reached the goal.

During the "trekking" trip from Cape Colony to the final settlement in the Transvaal the

Boer settlers shot no less than six thousand lions, and of that number Kruger is credited with shooting more than two hundred and fifty.

His personal bravery was never shown to better advantage than in 1857, when he was sub-commandant of the Transvaal army. He had ordered several of his burghers to go into the Orange Free State, with which country there was a serious misunderstanding, and there they were arrested. As soon as Mr. Kruger heard of the men's arrest he hastened into the camp of the Free State forces and asked for the release of the prisoners on the ground that they were innocent, and that if any one were guilty he was that man, because he had ordered them to enter the country. The commandant of the Free State forces was so greatly amazed by Mr. Kruger's bravery that he allowed all the Boers to return to their own camp.

Mr. Kruger's remarkable vitality and capacity for hard mental labour are the results of the great care which he bestows upon himself and the regular habits which he has followed for almost twenty years. He rises at half past five o'clock every morning, and follows a daily programme, from which he never deviates unless he is absent from home. After he leaves his bedroom he proceeds to his library and drinks several cups of intensely black coffee, and smokes several pipefuls of strong Boer tobacco. Then he spends the greater part of an hour in family devotions and the perusal of the Bible. After breakfast, at half past seven o'clock, he receives the members of the Volksraad, and then transacts the heaviest business of the day. After all the Volksraad members have departed, he steps out on the piazza of his little whitewashed cottage and joins the burghers, or citizens, who every morning congregate there and discuss state affairs while they sip the coffee and smoke the tobacco which the President furnishes to all visitors.

At ten o'clock the state carriage and its escort of eight gaudily apparelled troopers await him at the gate, and he is conveyed to the Government House, several blocks distant. As soon as he arrives there he is to be found either in one legislative chamber or the other, directing the affairs of the two bodies, making addresses or quietly watching the progress of legislative matters. At noon he returns to his home for luncheon, but is back at his duties in the Government House at two o'clock, and remains there three hours in the afternoon. Thereafter he receives burghers at his home until seven o'clock, and retires every evening at precisely eight o'clock.

The power which Mr. Kruger has over the majority of his countrymen is due in no small measure to his fondness for conversing with them and his treatment of them when they visit his cottage. As soon as the sun has risen, a small stream of Boers wends its way toward the President's cottage and awaits his appearance on the piazza. When Mr. Kruger comes among them he loses his identity as President, and merges his personality into that of an ordinary burgher. This custom has endeared him in the affections of his people, and, as a result, whenever he makes a stand on any question it may be taken for granted that he has thoroughly discussed the subject beforehand with his burghers, and that he can depend upon the majority of them for their support.

Mr. Kruger is a speech-maker of no mean ability. His addresses in the Volksraad are filled with good reasoning, homely similes, biblical quotations, and convincing argument. He speaks without preparation, indulges in no flights of oratory, but uses the simple, plain language that is easily understood by the burgher as well as the statesman. All his speeches are delivered in the Boer "taal," a dialect which bears the same relation to the Dutch language as "low" German does to "high" German. Generally the dialect is used by the Boers in speaking only, the pure Dutch being used in correspondence and official state papers.

The President may be able to speak the English language, but if such is the case he succeeds admirably in allowing no one except his most trusted friends to hear him. Much investigation has failed to reveal any one in Pretoria who has ever heard him speak the English language, although reports have it that he speaks it fluently. He understands the language well, and any one who has ever held a conversation with him through an interpreter will recall that he occasionally forgets his assumed inability to understand English, and replies to a question before the interpreter has commenced to translate it.

Mr. Kruger has been twice married. His first wife, a Miss Du Plessis, was the daughter of one of the early voortrekkers, and with the other women took part in many of the Boer wars against the natives. She died shortly after the founding of the republic, and left one son, who lived only a short time. Mr. Kruger several years afterward married his first wife's niece, who is now the first lady of the land. Like almost all Boer women, she has a retiring disposition, and very rarely appears in public except at religious gatherings. The President rarely introduces her to his visitors, probably in obedience to her own desires, but she constantly entertains the wives and daughters of burghers who call on her husband.

President and Madame Kruger have had sixteen children, seven of whom still live. One of his sons is the President's private secretary, and a youth of decidedly modern ideas and tendencies. Another son is a private in the

Pretoria police, a state military organization in which he takes great pride. A third occupies his father's farm near Rustenberg. The other children are daughters, who are married to Boer farmers and business men. One of Kruger's sons-in-law is Captain F. C. Eloff, who was taken prisoner by the Uitlanders during the raid, and who has since aroused the enmity of the English residents by freely expressing his opinion of them in public speeches. Captain Eloff is several times a millionaire, and lives in a two-hundred-and-fifty-thousand-dollar mansion.

Popular report in Pretoria has it that the President's wealth amounts to a million dollars, but his mode of living certainly does not betray it. His salary as President is thirty-five thousand dollars, in addition to which he is annually allowed fifteen hundred dollars for house-rent, or "huishuur." He has long since purchased the house in which he lives, but, as the allowance of fifteen hundred dollars is annually paid to him, the English residents aver that the amount is intended as a slight reimbursement to him for the money he spends for the coffee and tobacco used by the burgher callers at his cottage. During the later years of his life Barney Barnato, the wizard of South African finance, supplied to the President all the tobacco he used, and consequently Mr. Kruger was able to save the Government tobacco allowance. Barnato also presented to Mr. Kruger two handsome marble statues of lions which now adorn the lawn of the presidential residence. A photograph which is greatly admired by the patriotic Boers represents Mr. Kruger appropriately resting his hand on the head of one of the recumbent lions in a manner which to them suggests the physical superiority of the Boers over the British.

Mr. Kruger has always been a man of deep and earnest religious convictions. In his youth he was taught the virtues of a Christian life, and it is not recorded that he ever did anything which was inconsistent with his training. An old Zulu headman who lives near the Vaal River, in the Orange Free State, relates that Mr. Kruger yoked him beside an ox in a transport wagon when the trekkers departed from Natal in the early '40s, and compelled him to do the work of a beast; but he has no good reason for declaring that his bondsman was Mr. Kruger rather than any one of the other Boers in the party.

When Mr. Kruger was about thirty-five years old his religious enthusiasm led him into an experience which almost resulted in his death. He had met with some reverses, which caused him to doubt the genuineness of religious assistance. He endeavoured to find comfort and consolation in his Bible, but failed, and he became sorely troubled. One night, after bidding farewell to his wife, he disappeared into the wilderness of the Magalies Hills, a short distance west of Pretoria. After he had been absent from his home for several days, a number of men went to the hills to search for him, and found him on his knees engaged in singing and praying. He had been so many days without food and water that he was too weak to rise from the ground, and it was necessary for the men to carry him to his home. Since that experience he has believed himself to be a special instrument of a divine power, and by his deeds has given the impression that he is a leader chosen to defend the liberties and homes of his people.

He never speaks of his experience in the hills, but those who have been his friends for many years say that it marked an epoch in his life. The Boers, who have none of the modern cynicism and scepticism, regard him as the wielder of divine power, while those who admire nothing which he is capable of doing scoff and jeer at him as a religious fanatic, and even call him a hypocrite. Any one who has observed Mr. Kruger in his daily habits, or has heard him in the pulpit of the church opposite the cottage where he lives, will bear witness to the intensity and earnestness of his genuine religious feeling. The lessons of life which he draws from his own personal experiences, and expounds to his congregation with no little degree of earnestness, are of such a character as to remove all doubts which the mind may have concerning his purity of purpose.

Mr. Kruger's style of writing is unique, but thoroughly characteristic of himself. The many references to the Deity, the oftentimes pompous style, the words which breathe of the intense interest in and loyalty to his countrymen, all combine to make his state communications and proclamations most interesting reading. The following proclamation, made to the citizens of Johannesburg several days after the Jameson raid, is typical:

"*To all the Residents of Johannesburg.*

"I, S. J. P. Kruger, State President of the South African Republic, with the advice and consent of the Executive Council, by virtue of Article VI of the Minutes of the Council, dated January 10, 1896, do hereby make known to all the residents of Johannesburg and neighbourhood that I am inexpressibly thankful to God that the despicable and treacherous incursion into my country has been prevented, and the independence of the republic saved, through the courage and bravery of my burghers.

"The persons who have been guilty of this crime must naturally be punished according to law—that is to say, they must stand their trial before the high court and a jury—but there are thousands who have been misled and deceived, and it has clearly appeared to me that even among the so-called leaders of the movement there are many who have been deceived.

"A small number of intriguers in and outside of the country ingeniously incited a number of the residents of Johannesburg and surroundings to struggle, under the guise of standing up for political rights, and day by day, as it were, urged them on; and when in their stupidity they thought that the moment had arrived, they (the intriguers) caused one Dr. Jameson to cross the boundary of the republic.

"Did they ever ask themselves to what they were exposing you?

"I shudder when I think what bloodshed could have resulted had a merciful Providence not saved you and my burghers.

"I will not refer to the financial damage.

"Now I approach you with full confidence. Work together with the Government of this republic, and strengthen their hands to make this country a land wherein people of all nationalities may reside in common brotherhood.

"For months and months I have planned what changes and reforms could have been considered desirable in the Government and the state, but the loathsome agitation, especially of the press, has restrained me.

"The same men who have publicly come forward as leaders have demanded reforms from me, and in a tone and a manner which they would not have ventured to have done in their own country, owing to fear for the criminal law. For that cause it was made impossible for me and my burghers, the founders of this republic, to take their preposterous proposals in consideration.

"It is my intention to submit a draft law at the first ordinary session of the Raad, whereby a municipality, with a mayor at the head, would be granted to Johannesburg, to whom the control of the city will be intrusted. According to all constitutional principles, the Municipal Board will be elected by the people of the town.

"I earnestly request you, laying your hands on your hearts, to answer me this question: After what has happened, can and may I submit this to the representatives of the people? My reply is, I know there are thousands in

Johannesburg and the suburbs to whom I can intrust such elective powers. Inhabitants of Johannesburg, render it possible for the Government to go before the Volksraad with the motto, 'Forgotten and Forgiven.'"

Mr. Kruger's political platform is based on one of the paragraphs of a manifesto which he, as Vice-President of the Triumvirate, sent to Sir Owen Lanyon, the British Resident Commissioner, on Dingaan's Day, 1880, when the Boers were engaged in their second struggle for independence. The paragraph, which was apparently written by Mr. Kruger, reads:

"We declare before God, who knows the heart, and before the world: Any one speaking of us as rebels is a slanderer! The people of the South African Republic have never been subjects of Her Majesty, and never will be."

The President's hatred of the English was bred in the bone, and it will never be eradicated. To see his country free from every English tie is the aim of his existence, and every act of his political career has been born with that thought. His own political aggrandizement has always been a secondary thought. He himself has declared that there is no one in the republic who is able or willing to complete the independence of the republic with such little friction as he, and that, such being the case, he would be a traitor to desert the cause in the hours of its gravest peril. He considers personal victories at the polls of his own country as mere stepping-stones toward that greater victory which he hopes to secure over the English colonial secretary, and the day that England renounces all claim to suzerainty over the Transvaal Mr. Kruger will consider his duty done, and will go into the retirement which his great work and the fulness of his years owe him.

For a man whose education has been of the scantiest, and whose people were practically unheard of until he brought them into prominence, Paul Kruger has received from foreign sources many remarkable tributes to the wisdom with which he has conducted the affairs of the country under circumstances of more than ordinary difficulty.

That which he received from Emperor William, of Germany, several days after the repulse of the Jameson raiders, was perhaps the finest tribute that Mr. Kruger has ever received, and one that created a greater sensation throughout the world than any peaceful message that ever passed between the heads of two governments. The cablegram, of which the text follows, is one of the most priceless treasures in Mr. Kruger's collection:

"*Received January 3d, 1896.*
"*From Wilhelm I. R., Berlin.*
"*To* PRESIDENT KRUGER, *Pretoria.*

"I tender you my sincere congratulations that, without appealing to the help of friendly powers, you and your people have been successful in opposing with your own forces the armed bands that have broken into your country to disturb the peace, in restoring order, and in maintaining the independence of your country against attacks from without.

"WILHELM I. R."

Prince Bismarck declared that Kruger was the greatest natural-born statesman of the time.

William E. Gladstone, who had many opportunities to gauge Kruger's skill in diplomacy, referred to him as the shrewdest politician on the continent of Africa, and not a mean competitor of those of Europe. Among the titles which have been bestowed upon him by European rulers are Knight of the First Class of the Red Eagle of Prussia, Grand Officer of the Legion of Honour, Grand Knight of the Leopold Order of Belgium, Grand Knight of the Netherland Lion, and Grand Knight of the Portuguese Order of Distinguished Foreigners.

If a detailed history of Mr. Kruger's life could be obtained from his own lips, it would compare favourably with those of the notable characters of modern times. The victories he has gained in the field of diplomacy may not have affected as many people as those of Bismarck; the defeats administered in battle may not have been as crushing as those of Napoleon, but to his weakling country they were equally as decisive and valuable.

The great pyramid in the valley of the Nile is seen to best advantage as far away as Cairo. Observed close at hand, it serves only to disturb the spectator's mind with an indefinable sense of vastness, crudity, and weight; from a distance the relative proportions of all things are clearly discerned. So it is with the career of Mr. Kruger. Historic perspective is necessary to determine the value of the man to the country. Fifty or a hundred years hence, when the Transvaal has safely emerged from its period of danger, there will be a true sense of proportion, so that his labours in behalf of his country may be judged aright.

At this time the critical faculty is lacking because his life work is not ended, and its entire success is not assured. He has earned for himself, however, the distinction of being the greatest diplomatist that South Africa has ever produced. Whether the fruits of his diplomacy will avail to keep his country intact is a question that will find its answer in the results of future years. He has succeeded in doing that which no man has ever done. As the head of the earth's weakest nation he has for more than a decade defied its strongest power to take his country from him. That should be sufficient honour for any man.

CHAPTER VI

INTERVIEW WITH PRESIDENT KRUGER

As is the rule with them everywhere, Englishmen in South Africa speak of Mr. Kruger with contempt and derision. Unprejudiced Americans and other foreigners in South Africa admire him for his patriotism, his courage in opposing the dictatorial policy of England's Colonial Office, and his efforts to establish a republic as nearly like that of the United States of America as possible. My desire to see Mr. Kruger was almost obliterated a week after my arrival in the country by the words of condemnation which were heaped upon him by Englishmen whenever his name was mentioned. In nearly every Englishman's mind the name of "Oom Paul" was a synonym for all that was corrupt and vile; few gave him a word of commendation.

When I came into the pretty little town

of Pretoria, the capital of the Transvaal, where the President lives and where he mingles daily with the populace with as much freedom and informality as a country squire, there was a rapid transformation in my opinion of the man. The Boers worship their leader; to them he is a second George Washington, and even a few Englishmen there speak with admiration of him.

The day before my arrival in the town John McCann, of Johannesburg, who is a former New-Yorker and a friend of the President, informed Mr. Kruger of my intention to visit Pretoria. The President had refused interviews to three representatives of influential London newspapers who had been in the town three months waiting for the opportunity, but he expressed a desire to see an American.

"The Americans won't lie about me," he said to Mr. McCann. "I want America to learn our side of the story from me. They have had only the English point of view." I had scarcely reached my hotel when an emissary from the President called and made an appointment for me to meet him in the afternoon. The emissary conducted me to the Government Building, where the Volksraad was in session, and it required only a short time for it to become known that a representative from the great sister republic across the Atlantic desired to learn the truth about the Boers.

I was overwhelmed with information. Cabinet members, Raad members, the Commissioner of War, the Postmaster General, the most honoured and influential men of the republic —men who had more than once risked their lives in fighting for their country's preservation—gathered around me and were so eager to have me tell America of the wrongs they had suffered at the hands of the British that the scene was highly pathetic.

One after another spoke of the severe trials through which their young republic had passed, the efforts that had been made to disrupt it, and the constant harassment to which they had been subjected by enemies working under the cloak of friendship. The majority spoke English, but such as knew only the Boer taal were given an opportunity by their more fortunate friends to add to the testimony, and spoke through an interpreter. Such earnest, such honest conversation it had never been my lot to hear before. It was a memorable hour that I spent listening to the plaints of those plain, good-hearted Boers in the heart of South Africa. It was the voice of the downtrodden, the weak crying out against the strong.

When the hour of my appointment with the President arrived there was a unanimous desire among the Boers gathered around to accompany me. It was finally decided by them that six would be a sufficient number, and among those chosen were Postmaster-General Van Alpen, who was a representative at the Postal Congress in Washington several years ago; Commissioner of Mines P. Kroebler, Commissioner of War J. J. Smidt, Justice of the Peace Dillingham, and former Commandant-General Stephanne Schoeman.

When our party reached the little whitewashed cottage in which the President lives a score or more of tall and soil-stained farmers were standing in a circular group on the low-piazza. They were laughing hilariously at something that had been said by a shorter, fat man who was nearly hidden from view by the surrounding circle of patriarchs. A breach in the circle disclosed the President of the republic with his left arm on the shoulder of a long-whiskered Boer, and his right hand swinging lightly in the hand of another of his countrymen. It was democracy in its highest exemplification.

Catching a glimpse of us as we were entering on the lawn, the President hastily withdrew into the cottage. The Boers he deserted seated themselves on benches and chairs on the piazza, relighted their pipes, and puffed contentedly, without paying more attention to us than to nod to several of my companions as we passed them.

The front door of the cottage, or "White House," as they call it, was wide open. There was no flunkey in livery to take our cards, no white-aproned servant girls to tra-la-la our names. The executive mansion of the President was as free and open to visitors as the farmhouse of the humblest burgher of the re-

INTERVIEW WITH PRESIDENT KRUGER

public. In their efforts to display their qualities of politeness my companions urged me into the President's private reception room, while they lingered for a short time at the threshold. The President rose from his chair in the opposite end, met me in the centre of the room, and had grasped my hand before my companions had an opportunity of going through the process of an introduction.

There was less formality and red tape in meeting "Oom Paul" than would be required to have a word with Queen Victoria's butcher or President McKinley's office-boy.

While Mr. Kruger's small fat hand was holding mine in its grasp and shaking it vehemently, he spoke something in Boer, to which I replied, "Heel goed, danke," meaning "Very well, I thank you." Some one had told me that he would first ask concerning my health, and also gave me the formula for an answer. The President laughed heartily at my reply, and made a remark in Boer "taal." The interpreter came up in the meantime and straightened out the tangle by telling me that the President's first question had been "Have you any English blood in your veins?"

The President, still laughing at my reply, seated himself in a big armchair at the head of a table on which was a heavy pipe and a large tobacco box. He filled the pipe, lighted the tobacco, and blew great clouds of smoke toward the ceiling. My companions took turns in filling their pipes from the President's tobacco box, and in a few minutes the smoke was so dense as nearly to obscure my view of the persons in front of me.

The President crossed his short, thin legs and blew quick, spirited puffs of smoke while an interpreter translated to him my expression of the admiration which the American people had for him, and how well known the title "Oom Paul" was in America. This delighted the old man immeasurably. His big, fat body seemed to resolve itself into waves which started in his shoes and gradually worked upward until the fat rings under his eyes hid the little black orbits from view. Then he slapped his knees with his hands, opened his large mouth, and roared with laughter.

It was almost a minute before he regained his composure sufficiently to take another puff at the pipe which is his constant companion. During the old man's fit of laughter one of my companions nudged me and advised me: "Now ask him anything you wish. He is in better humour than I have ever seen him before." The President checked a second outburst of laughter rather suddenly and asked, "Are you a friend of Cecil Rhodes?" If there is any one whom "Oom Paul" detests it is the great colonizer. The President invariably asks this question of strangers, and if the answer is an affirmative one he refuses to continue the conversation.

Being assured that such was not the case, Mr. Kruger's mind appeared to be greatly relieved—as he is very suspicious of all strangers—and he asked another question which is indicative of the religious side of his nature: "To what Church do you belong?" A speaking acquaintanceship was claimed with the Dutch Reformed Church, of which the President is a most devout member, and this served to dissipate all suspicions he might have had concerning me.

The interpreter was repeating a question to him when the President suddenly interrupted, as is frequently his custom during a conversation, and asked: " Do the American people know the history of our people? I will tell you truthfully and briefly. You have heard the English version always; now I will give you ours."

The President proceeded slowly and, between puffs at his great pipe, spoke determinedly: " When I was a child we were so maltreated by the English in Cape Colony that we could no longer bear the abuses to which we were subjected. In 1835 we migrated northward with our cattle and possessions and settled in Natal, just south of Zululand, where by unavoidable fighting we acquired territory from the Zulus. We had hardly settled that country and established ourselves and a local form of government when our old enemies followed, and by various high-handed methods made life so unendurable that we were again compelled to move our families and possessions. This time we travelled five hundred miles inland over the trackless veldt and across the Vaal River, and after many hardships and trials settled in the Transvaal. The country was so poor, so uninviting, that the English colonists did not think it worth their while to settle in the land which we had chosen for our abiding-place.

" Our people increased in number, and, as the years passed, established a form of government such as yours in America. The British thought they were better able to govern us than we were ourselves, and once took our country from us. Their defeats at Laing's Nek and Majuba Hill taught them that we were fighters, and they gave us our independence and allowed us to live peaceably for a number of years. They did not think the country valuable enough to warrant the repetition of the fighting for it. When it became known all over the world twelve years ago that the most extensive gold fields on the globe had been discovered in our apparently worthless country, England became envious and laid plans to annex such a valuable prize. Thousands of people were attracted hither by our wonderful gold mines at Johannesburg, and the English statesmen renewed their attacks on us. They made all sorts of pretexts to rob us of our country, and when they could not do it in a way that was honest and would be commended by other nations, they planned the Jameson raid, which was merely a bold attempt to steal our country."

At this point Kruger paused for a moment and then added, "You Americans know how well they succeeded." This sally amused him and my companions hugely, and they all joined in hearty laughter.

The President declared that England's attitude toward them had changed completely since the discovery of the gold fields. "Up to that time we had been living in harmony with every one. We always tried to be peaceable and to prevent strife between our neighbours, but we have been continually harassed since the natural wealth of our land has been uncovered."

Here he relighted his pipe, which had grown cold while he was detailing the history of the Transvaal Boers, and then drew a parable, which is one of his distinguishing traits: "The gold fields may be compared to a pretty girl who is young and wealthy. You all admire her and want her to be yours, but when she rejects you your anger rises and you want to destroy her." By implication England is the rejected suitor, and the Transvaal the rich young girl.

Comparing the Boers' conduct in South Africa with that of the English, the President said: "Ever since we left Cape Colony in 1835 we have not taken any territory from the natives by conquest except that of one chief whose murderous maraudings compelled us to drive him away from his country. We bartered and bought every inch of land we now have. England has taken all the land she has in South Africa at the muzzles of repeating rifles and machine guns. That is the civilized method of extending the bounds of the empire they talk about so much."

The Englishmen's plaint is that the republic will tax them, but allow them no representation in the affairs of government. The

President explained his side in this manner: "Every man, be he Englishman, Chinaman, or Eskimo, can become a naturalized citizen of our country and have all the privileges of a burgher in nine years. If we should have a war, a foreigner can become a citizen in a minute if he will fight with our army. The difficulty with the Englishmen here is that they want to be burghers and at the same time retain their English citizenship.

"A man can not serve two masters; either he will hate the one and love the other, or hold to the one and despise the other. We have a law for bigamy in our country, and it is necessary to dispose of an old love before it is possible to marry a new."

"Oom Paul" is very bitter in his feeling against the English, whom he calls his natural enemies, but it is seldom that he says anything against them except in private to his most intimate friends. The present great distress in the Johannesburg gold fields is attributed by the English residents to the high protective duties imposed by the Government and the high freight charges for the transmission of machinery and coal. Mr. Kruger explained that those taxes were less than in the other colonies in the country.

"We are high protectionists because ours is a young country. These new mines have cost the Government great amounts of money, and it is necessary for us to raise as much as we expend. They want us to give them everything gratuitously, so that we may become bankrupt and they can take our country for the debt. If they don't like our laws, why don't they stay away?"

Nowhere in the world is the American Republic admired as much outside of its own territory as in South Africa. Both the Transvaal and the Orange Free State Constitutions are patterned after that of the United States, and there is a desire lurking in the breasts of thousands of South Africans to convert the whole of the country south of the Zambezi into one grand United States of South Africa.

Sir Alfred Milner, the Queen's Commissioner to South Africa, said to me several days before I saw Mr. Kruger that such a thing might come to pass within the next twenty years. The President hesitated when I asked him if he favoured such a proposition to unite all the colonies and republics in the country. "If I should say 'Yes,' the English would declare war on us to-morrow." He appeared to be very cautious on this subject for a few minutes, but after a consultation with my companions, he spoke more freely.

"We admire your Government very much," he said, "and think there is none better in the world. At the present time there are so many conflicting affairs in this country as to make the discussion of an amalgamation inadvisable. A republic formed on the principle of the United States would be most advantageous to all concerned, but South Africa is not yet ripe for such a government. I shall not live to see it."

According to those around him, the President had not been in such a talkative mood for a long time, and, acting upon that information, I asked him to tell me concerning the Boers' ability to defend themselves in case of war with England. Many successes against British arms have caused the Boers to regard their prowess very highly, and they generally speak of themselves as well able to protect their country. The two countries have been on the very verge of war several times during the last three years, and it was only through the greatest diplomacy that the thousands of English soldiers were not sent over the border of the Transvaal, near which they have been stationed ever since the memorable raid of Jameson's troopers.

The President's reply was guarded: "The English say they can starve us out of our country by placing barriers of soldiers along the borders. Starve us they can, if it is the will of God that such should be our fate. If God is on our side they can build a big wall around us and we can still live and flourish. We don't want war. My wish is to live in peace with everybody."

It was evident that the subject was not pleasant to him, and he requested me to ask Commissioner of War Smidt, a war-scarred hero of Majuba Hill, to speak to me on the ability of the Boers to take care of themselves in case of a conflict.

. Commissioner Smidt became very enthusiastic as he progressed with the expression of his opinion, and the President frequently nodded assent to what the head of the War Department said.

"It is contrary to our national feeling to engage in war," said Mr. Smidt, "and we will do all in our power to avert strife. If, however, we are forced into fighting, we must defend ourselves as best we are able. There is not one Boer in the Transvaal who will not fight until death for his country. We have demonstrated our ability several times, and we shall try to retain our reputation. The English must fight us in our own country, where we know every rock, every valley, and every hill. They fight at a disadvantage in a country which they do not know and in a climate to which they are strangers.

"The Boers are born sharpshooters, and from infancy are taught to put a bullet in a buzzard's skull at a hundred yards. One Boer is equal in a war in our own country to five Englishmen, and that has been proved a number of times. We have rugged constitutions,

INTERVIEW WITH PRESIDENT KRUGER 153

are accustomed to an outdoor life, and can live on a piece of biltong for days, while the Queen's soldiers have none of these advantages.

"They can not starve us out in fifty years, for we have sources of provender of which they can not deprive us. We have fortifications around Pretoria that make it an impossibility for any army of less than fifty thousand men to take, and the ammunition we have on hand is sufficient for a three years' war. We are not afraid of the English in Africa, and not until every Boer in the Transvaal is killed will we stop fighting if they ever begin. Should war come, and I pray that it will not, the Boers will march through English territory to the Cape of Good Hope, or be erased from the face of the earth."

Never was a man more sincere in his statements than the commissioner, and his companions supported his every sentence by look and gesture. Even the President gave silent approval to the sentiments expressed.

"Have you ever had any intention of securing Delagoa Bay from the Portuguese, in order that you might have a seacoast, as has been rumoured many times?" I asked the President. Delagoa Bay, the finest harbour in Africa, is within a few miles of the Transvaal, and might be of great service to it in the event of war.

"'Cursed be he who removes the landmarks of his neighbour,'" quoted he. "I never want to do anything that would bring the vengeance of God on me. We want our country, nothing more, nothing less."

Asked to give an explanation of the causes of the troubles between England and the Transvaal, he said:

"Mr. Rhodes is the cause of all the troubles between our country and England. He desires to form all the country south of the Zambezi River into a United States of South Africa, and before he can do this he must have possession of the Transvaal and the Orange Free State. His aim in life is to be President of the United States of South Africa. He initiated the Jameson raid, and he has stirred up the spirit of discontent which is being shown by the Englishmen in the Transvaal. Our Government endeavours to treat every one with like favour, but these Englishmen are never satisfied with anything we do. They want the English flag to wave over the Transvaal territory, and nothing less. Rhodes spent millions of pounds in efforts to steal our country, and will probably spend millions more. But we will never leave this land, which we found, settled, and protected."

Then, rising from his chair and raising his voice, he continued slowly and deliberately:

"We will fight until not one Boer remains to defend our flag and country; our women and children will fight for their liberties; and even I, an old man, will take the gun which I have used against them twice before and use it again to defend the country I love. But I hope there will be no war. I want none and the Boers want none. If war comes, we shall not be to blame. I have done all in my power for peace, and have taken many insults from Englishmen merely that my people might not be plunged into war. I want no war. I hope that I may spend the rest of my days in peace."

The President's carriage had arrived in

front of the cottage to convey him to the Government Building, and the time had arrived for him to appear before one of the Volksraads. He displayed no eagerness to end the interview, and continued it by asking me to describe the personality and ability of President McKinley. He expressed his admiration of former President Cleveland, with whose Department of State he had some dealings while John Hays Hammond was confined in the Pretoria prison for complicity in the Jameson raid.

His opinion of the Americans in South Africa was characteristic of the man. " I like and trust true Americans. They are a magnificent people, because they favour justice. When those in our country are untainted with English ideas I trust them implicitly, but there were a number of them here in Jameson's time who were Americans in name only."

He hesitated to send any message to the sister republic in America, lest his English enemies might construe it to mean that he curried America's favour. His friends finally persuaded him to make a statement, and he dictated this expression of good fellowship and respect:

"So long as the different sections of the United States live in peace and harmony, so long will they be happy and prosperous. My wish is that the great republic in America may become the greatest nation on earth, and that she may continue to act as the great peace nation. I wish that prosperity may be hers and her people's, and in my daily prayers I ask that God may protect her and bless her bounteously."

It being far past the time for his appearance at the Government Building, the President ended the interview abruptly. He refilled his pipe, bade farewell to us, and bustled from the room with all the vigour of a young man. On the piazza he met his little, silver-haired wife, who, with a half-knit stocking pendant from her fingers, was conversing with the countrymen sitting on the benches. The President bent down and kissed her affectionately, then jumped into the carriage and was rapidly conveyed to the Government Building. When the dust obscured the carriage and the cavalrymen attending it, one of my companions turned to me and remarked:

"Ah! there goes a great man!"

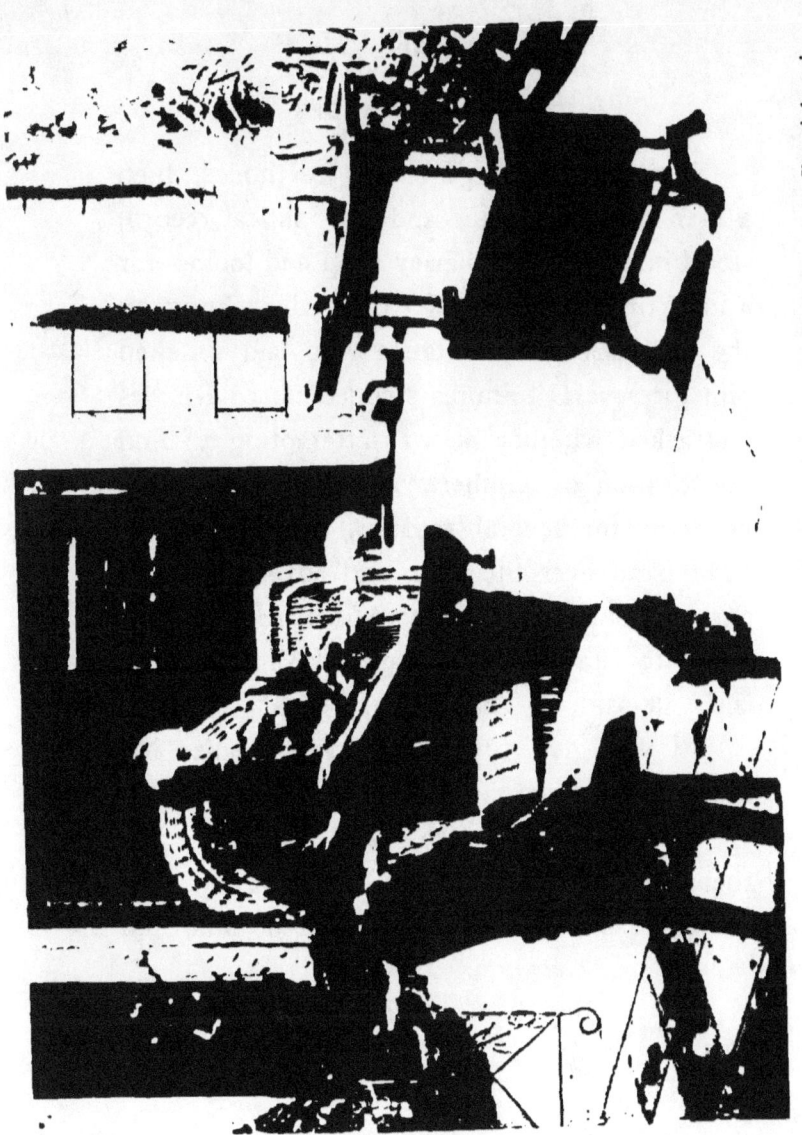

The Rt. Hon. Cecil J. Rhodes on the piazza of his residence, Groote Schuur, at Rondebosch, near Cape Town.

CHAPTER VII

CECIL JOHN RHODES

SIXTEEN years ago Cecil J. Rhodes, then a man of small means and no political record, stood in a small Kimberley shop and looked for a long time at a map of Africa which hung on the wall. An acquaintance who had watched him for several minutes stepped up to Rhodes and asked whether he was attempting to find the location of Kimberley. Mr. Rhodes made no reply for several seconds, then placed his right hand over the map, and covered a large part of South and Central Africa from the Atlantic to the Indian Ocean. "All that British!" he said. "That is my dream."

"I will give you ten years to realize it," replied the friend.

"Give me ten more," said Rhodes, "and then we'll have a new map."

Three fourths of the required time has

elapsed, and the full realization of Rhodes's dream must take place within the next four years. There remain only two small spaces on that part of the map which was covered by Rhodes's hand that are not British, and those are the Orange Free State and the South African Republic. Mr. Rhodes's success will come hand-in-hand with the death of the two republics. The life of the republics hinges on his failure, and good fortune has rarely deserted him.

Twenty-seven years ago Cecil Rhodes, then a tall, thin college lad, was directed by his physician to go to South Africa if he wished to live more than three years. He and his brother Herbert, the sons of the poor rector of Bishop Stortford, sailed for Durban, Natal, and reached that port while the diamond fever was at its height at Kimberley. The two boys, each less than nineteen years old, joined a party of adventurers and prospectors, and, after many vicissitudes, reached the Kimberley fields safely, but with little or no money. The boys were energetic, and found opportunities for making money where others could see none.

The camp was composed of the roughest characters in South Africa, all of whom had flocked thither when the discovery of diamonds was first announced. Illicit diamond buying was the easiest path to wealth, and was travelled by almost every millionaire whose name has been connected with recent South African affairs. Mr. Rhodes is one of the few exceptions, and even his enemies corroborate the statement.

"You don't steal diamonds," said Barney Barnato to Mr. Rhodes fifteen years ago, "but you must prove it when accused. I steal them, but my enemies must prove it. That's the difference between us."

The youthful Rhodes engaged in many legitimate schemes for making money, and saved almost all that he secured. For a short time he pumped water out of mines, using an abandoned engine for the purpose, and then embarked in commercial enterprises. After spending two or three years in the fields, he returned to England and resumed his course at Oxford. In connection with this visit to England, Mr. Rhodes relates the story of the meeting with the physician who several years before had placed the limit of his existence at three years.

"You the same Rhodes?" asked the discomfited doctor when he saw the healthy young man. "According to my books, you have been in your grave some time. Here is the entry: 'Tuberculosis; recovery impossible.' You can't be the same Rhodes, sir. Impossible!"

At the end of each term at Oxford Mr. Rhodes returned to Kimberley, and, by judiciously investing his savings in mining claims, soon became a power in the affairs of the diamond fields. When the diamond fever was followed by the usual reaction, and evil days fell upon the industry, Mr. Rhodes secured all the shares, claims, and lands that his thousands would buy. Then he conceived the idea of making a monopoly of the diamond industry by consolidating all the mines and limiting the output.

Lacking the money wherewith to buy the valuable properties necessary for his plans, he went to the Rothschilds and asked for financial assistance. The scheme was extraordinary, and required such a large amount of money that the request, coming from such a young man as Mr. Rhodes was then, staggered the Rothschilds, and they asked him to call several days later for an answer.

"My time is valuable," remarked Mr. Rhodes, rather haughtily. "I will come again in an hour for your answer. If you have not decided by that time, I shall seek assistance elsewhere."

The Rothschilds sent Mr. Rhodes back to Africa with the necessary amount of money to purchase the other claims and property in the Kimberley district, and, after he had formed the great De Beers Company, appointed him managing director for life at a salary of one hundred and fifty thousand dollars a year. Under Mr. Rhodes's management the De Beers consolidated mines have been earning annual dividends of almost fifty per cent., and more than four hundred million dollars' worth of diamonds have been placed on the market. With the exception of the Suez Canal, the mines are the best paying property in the world, and much of their success is due to the personal efforts of Mr. Rhodes.

It was while he was engineering the consolidation of the diamond mines that Mr. Rhodes began his political career. He realized that his political success was founded on personal popularity, and more firmly so in a new country, where the political elements were of such a diversified character as are usually present in a mining community. In the early days of the Kimberley fields the extent of a man's popularity depended upon the amount of money he spent in wining those around him. Mr. Rhodes was astute enough to appreciate the secret of popularity, and, having gained it, allowed himself to be named as candidate for the Cape Colony Parliament from the Kimberley district.

By carefully currying the favour of the Dutch inhabitants, who were not on the friendliest political terms with the English colonists, he was elected. Thereafter Mr. Rhodes's political star was in the ascendant, and he was elected successively to the highest office in the colony's government.

At the age of twenty-eight he was Treasurer-General of Cape Colony, and it was while he filled that office that Chinese Gordon appeared at the Cape and appealed to Mr. Rhodes to join the expedition to Khartoum. Mr. Rhodes was undecided whether to resign the treasurer-generalship and accompany Gordon or to remain in South Africa, but finally determined to stay in the colony. Gordon, who had taken a great fancy to the young and energetic colonist, was sorely disappointed, and went to Khartoum, where he was killed.

During the years he held minor Government offices Mr. Rhodes formed the alliances which were the foundation of his later political success. He was a friend at the same time of the Englishman, the Afrikander, the Dutchman, and the Boer, and he was always in a position where he could reciprocate the favours of one class without incurring the enmity of another. He worked with the Dutchmen when protection was the political cry, and with the Englishmen when subjects dear to them were in the foreground. He never abused his opponents in political arguments, as the majority of Cape politicians do, but he pleaded with them on the veldt and at their firesides.

When he was unable to swerve a man's opinions by words, he has frequently been charged with having applied the more seductive method of using money. Mr. Rhodes is said to be a firm believer in money as a force superior to all others, and he does not hesitate to acknowledge his belief that every man's opinions can be shaped by the application of a necessary amount of money. This belief he formed in the early days of the diamond fields, and it has remained with him ever since.

"Find the man's price" was Mr. Rhodes's formula for success before he reached the age of thirty, and his political enemies declare it has given him the power he desired. In a country which had such a large roving and reckless population as South Africa it was not difficult for a politician with a motto similar to that of Mr. Rhodes's to become influential at election periods, nor did it require many years to establish a party that would support him on whatever grounds he chose to take.

It was with such a following that Mr.

Rhodes commenced his higher political career in Cape Colony. When, in 1884, he became Commissioner of Bechuanaland, the vast and then undeveloped country adjoining the colony on the north, and made his first plans for the annexation of that territory to the British Empire, he received the support of the majority of the voters of the colony. His first plan of securing control of the territory was not favourably received by the Colonial Office in London, and no sooner was it pronounced visionary than he suggested another more feasible.

Bechuanaland was then ruled by a mighty native chief, Lobengula, whose vast armies roved over the country and prevented white travellers and prospectors from crossing the bounds of his territory. In the minds of the white people of South Africa, Bechuanaland figured as a veritable Golconda—a land where precious stones and minerals could be secured without any attendant labour, where the soil was so rich as to yield four bounteous harvests every year.

Mr. Rhodes determined to break the barriers which excluded white men from the native chief's domain, and sent three agents to treat with Lobengula. The agents made many valuable presents to the old chief, and in 1888, after much engineering, secured from him an exclusive concession to search for and extract minerals in Bechuanaland. The payment for the concession included five hundred dollars a month, a thousand rifles and ammunition, and a small gunboat on the Zambezi.

After Mr. Rhodes discovered the real value of the concession, he and a number of his friends formed the British South Africa Company, popularly known as the Chartered Company, and received a charter from the British Government, which gave to them the exclusive right of governing, developing, and trading in Lobengula's country. Several years afterward the white man's government became irksome to Lobengula and his tribes, as well as to the Mashonas, who occupied the immense territory adjoining Bechuanaland on the east, and all rebelled. The result was not unlike those of native rebellions in other countries. The natives were shot down by trained English soldiers, their country was taken from them, and those who escaped death or captivity were compelled to fly for safety to the new countries of the north.

The British South Africa Company in 1895 practically became the sole owner of Rhodesia, the great territory taken from Lobengula and the Mashonas; and Mr. Rhodes, having realized part of his dream, began casting about for other opportunities whereby he might extend the empire.

Mr. Rhodes was then in the zenith of his glory. He was many times a millionaire, the head of one of the greatest capitalistic enterprises in the world, the director of the affairs of a dominion occupying one tenth of a continent, and the Premier of Cape Colony. His power was almost absolute over a territory that stretches from the Cape of Good Hope into Central Africa, and then eastward to within a few miles of the Indian Ocean. He had armies under his command, and two governments were at his beck and call.

But Mr. Rhodes was not satisfied. He looked again at the map of Africa, already greatly changed since he placed his hand over it in the Kimberley shop, but the dream was not realized. He saw the Transvaal and the Orange Free State flags still occupying the positions he had marked for the British emblem, and he plotted for their acquisition.

The strife between the Boers and the Uitlanders in the Transvaal was then at its height, and Mr. Rhodes recognised the opportunity for the intervention of England that it afforded. Mr. Rhodes did not consider it of sufficient importance to inquire concerning the justice of the Uitlanders' claims, nor did he express any sympathy for their cause. In fact, if anything, he felt that if the Uitlanders were unjustly treated by the Boers their remedy was simple. Once he blandly told a complaining Uitlander that no Chinese wall surrounded the Transvaal, and that to escape from the alleged injustice was comparatively easy.

To Mr. Rhodes the end was sufficient excuse for the means, and, if the acquisition of the two republics carried with it the loss of his Boer friends, he was willing to accept the situation. The fall of the Transvaal Republic carried with it the subsequent fall of the Orange

Free State, and, in order that he might strike at the head, he determined to commence his campaign of exterminating republics by first attacking the Transvaal.

Whether he had the promise of assistance from the Colonial Office in London is a subject upon which even the principals differ. Mr. Rhodes felt that his power in the country was great enough to make the attack upon the Transvaal without assistance from the home Government, and the plot of the Jameson raid was formed.

He retired to Groote Schuur, his home at Cape Town, and awaited the fruition of the plans he had so carefully made and explained. His lieutenants might have been overhasty, or perhaps the Uitlanders in Johannesburg might have feared the Boer guns too much; whatever the reason, the plans miscarried, and Mr. Rhodes experienced the first and greatest reverse in his brilliant public career.

The dream which appeared so near realization one day was dissolved the next, and with it the reputation of the dreamer. He was obliged to resign the premiership of Cape Colony, many of his best and oldest supporters in England deserted him, and he lost the respect and esteem of the Dutch inhabitants of South Africa, who had always been among his stanchest allies. The heroic Rhodes, the idol of Cape Colony, found himself the object of attack and ridicule of the majority of the voters of the colony. The parliamentary inquiry acquitted him of all complicity in the Jameson raid, it is true, but the Dutch people of South Africa never have and never will.

The Jameson raid was a mere incident in Mr. Rhodes's career; he would probably call it an accident. Having failed to overthrow the Transvaal Republic by means of an armed revolution, he attempted to accomplish the same object by means of a commercial revolution. Rhodesia, the new country which had a short time previously been taken from the Matabeles and the Mashonas, was proclaimed by Mr. Rhodes to be a paradise for settlers and an Ophir for prospectors. He personally conducted the campaign to rob the Transvaal of its inhabitants and its commerce; but the golden promises, the magnificent farms, the Solomon's mines, the new railways, and the new telegraph lines all failed to attract the coveted prizes to the land which, after all, was found to be void of real merit except as a hunting ground where the so-called British poor-house, the army, might pot negroes.

Mr. Rhodes spent hundreds of thousands of dollars in developing the country which bears his name, and the British South Africa Company added thousands more, but the hand which was wont to turn into gold all that it touched had lost its cunning. To add to Mr. Rhodes's perplexities, the natives who had been conquered by Dr. Jameson learned that their conqueror had been taken prisoner by the Boers, and rose in another rebellion against English authority. Mr. Rhodes and one of his sisters journeyed alone into the enemy's stronghold and made terms with Lobengula, whereby the revolution was practically ended.

After the Rhodesian country had been pacified, and he had placed the routine work of the campaign to secure settlers for the country in the hands of his lieutenants, Mr. Rhodes bent all his energies toward the completion of the transcontinental railway and telegraph lines which had been started under his auspices several years before, but had been allowed to lag on account of the pressure of weightier matters. The Cape Town to Cairo railroad and telegraph are undertakings of such vast proportions and importance that Mr. Rhodes's fame might easily have been secured through them alone had he never been heard of in connection with other great enterprises.

He himself originated the plans by which the Mediterranean and Table Bay will eventually be united by bands of steel and strands of copper, and it is through his own personal efforts that the English financiers are being induced to subscribe the money with which his plans are being carried out. The marvellous faith which the English people have in Mr. Rhodes has been illustrated on several occasions when he was called to London to meet storms of protests from shareholders, who feared that the two great enterprises were gigantic fiascos. He has invariably returned to South Africa with the renewed confidence of the timid ones and many millions of additional capital.

Mr. Rhodes has tasted of the power which is absolute, and he will brook no earthly interference with his plans. The natives may destroy hundreds of miles of the telegraph lines, as they have done on several occasions. He teaches them a lesson by means of the quick-firing gun, and rebuilds the line. White men may fear the deadly fever of Central Africa, but princely salaries and life-insurance policies for a host of relatives will always attract men to take the risk. Shareholders may rebel at the expenditures, but Mr. Rhodes will indicate to them that their other properties will be ruined if they withdraw their support from the railway and telegraph.

A strip of territory belonging to another nation may be an impediment to the line, but an interview with the Emperor of Germany or the King of Portugal will be all-sufficient for the accomplishment of Mr. Rhodes's purpose. Providence may swerve him in his purpose many times, but nations and individuals rarely.

All South Africans agree that Mr. Rhodes

is the most remarkable Englishman that ever figured in the history of the African continent. Some will go further and declare that he has done more for the British Empire than any one man in history. No two South Africans will agree on the methods by which Mr. Rhodes attained his position in the affairs of the country. Some say that he owes his success to his great wealth; others declare that his personal magnetism is responsible for all that he ever attained. His enemies intimate that political chicanery is the foundation of his progress, while his friends resent the intimation and laud his sterling honesty as the basis of his successful career.

No one has ever accused him of being the fortunate victim of circumstances which carried him to the pre-eminent rank he occupies among Englishmen, although such an opinion might readily be formed from a personal study of the man. South Africa is the indolent man's paradise, and of that garden of physical inactivity Mr. Rhodes, by virtue of his pre-eminent qualifications, is king. "Almost as lazy as Rhodes" is a South Africanism that has caused lifelong enmities and rivers of blood.

He takes pride in his indolence, and declares that the man who performs more labour than his physical needs demand is a fool. He says he never makes a long speech because he is too lazy to expend the energy necessary for its delivery. He declines to walk more than an eighth of a mile unless it is impossible to secure a vehicle or native hammock-bearers to convey him, and then he proceeds so slowly that his progress is almost imperceptible. His indolence may be the result of the same line of reasoning as that indulged in by the cautious man who carries an umbrella when the sun shines, in which case every one who has travelled in the tropics will agree that Mr. Rhodes is a modern Solomon. The only exercise he indulges in is an hour's canter on horseback in the early morning, before the generous rays of the African sun appear.

Notwithstanding his antipathy to physical exertion, Mr. Rhodes is a great traveller, and is constantly moving from one place to another. One week may find him at Groote

Schuur, his Cape Town residence, while the following week he may be planning a new farm in far-away Mashonaland. The third week may have him in the Portuguese possessions on the east coast, and at the end of the month he may be back in Cape Town, prepared for a voyage to England and a fortnight's stay in Paris. He will charter a bullock team or a steamship with like disregard of expense in order that he may reach his destination at a specified time, and in like manner he will be watchful of his comfort by causing houses to be built in unfrequented territory which he may wish to investigate.

So wealthy that he could almost double his fortune in the time it would require to count it, Mr. Rhodes is a firm believer in the doctrine that money was created for the purpose of being spent, and never hesitates to put it into practice. He does not assist beggars, nor does he squander sixpence in a year, but he will pay the expenses of a trip to Europe for a man whom he wishes to reconcile, and will donate the value of a thousand-acre farm to a tribe of natives which has pleased him by its actions.

His generosity is best illustrated by a story told by one of his most intimate friends in Kimberley. Several years before Barney Barnato's death, that not-too-honest speculator induced almost all of the employees of the diamond mines to invest their savings in the stock of the Pleiades gold mine in Johannesburg, which Barnato and his friends were attempting to manipulate. The attempt was unsuccessful, and the diamond miners lost all the money they had invested. Mr. Rhodes heard of Barnato's deceit, and asked him to refund the money, but was laughed at. Mr. Rhodes learned the total amount of the losses—about twenty-five thousand dollars—and paid the money out of his own pocket.

Although he has more financial patronage at his command than almost any banking house in existence, Mr. Rhodes rarely has sufficient money in his purse to buy lunch. His valet, a half-breed Malay named Tony, is his banker, and from him he is continually borrowing money. It is related that on a voyage to England he offered to make a wager of money, but found that he had nothing less valuable than a handful of loose rough diamonds in his trousers pocket.

Mr. Rhodes is an eloquently silent man. He talks little, but his paucity of words is no criterion of their weight. He can condense a chapter into a word, and a book into a sentence. The man whose hobby is to run an empire is almost as silent as the Sphinx in the land toward which that empire is being elongated. His sentences are short and curt. "I want a railroad here," or "We want this mine," or "We must have this strip of land," are common examples of his style of speech and the expression of his dominant spirit.

He has the faculty of leading people to believe that they want the exact opposite of what they really want, and he does it in such a polished manner that they give their consent before they realize what he has asked them. His personal charm, which in itself is almost irresistible, is fortified with a straightforward, breezy heartiness, that carries with it respect, admiration, confidence, and, finally, conviction. He has argued and treated with persons ranging in intelligence and station from a native chief to the most learned diplomats and rulers in the world, and his experience has taught him that argument will win any case.

Lobengula called him "the brother who eats a whole country for his dinner." To this title might be added "the debater who swallows up the opposition in one breath." Mr. Rhodes never asks exactly what he wants. He will ask the shareholders of a company for ten million, when he really needs only five million, but in that manner he is almost certain of satisfying his needs. In the same way when he pleads with an opponent he makes the demands so great that he can afford to yield half and still attain his object. Twelve years ago Mr. Rhodes demanded the appointment of Prime Minister of the Colony, but he was satisfied with the Commissionership of Crown Lands and Works, the real object of his aim.

If Mr. Rhodes had cast his lines in America instead of South Africa, he would be called a political boss. He would be the dominant factor of one of the parties, and he would be able to secure delegates with as much ease as he does in Cape Colony, where the population is less mixed than in our country. His political lieutenants act with the same vigour and on the same general lines as those in our country, and if a close examination of their work could be made, many political tricks that the American campaigner never heard of would probably be disclosed.

One of the mildest accusations against him is that he paid fifty thousand dollars for the support that first secured for him a seat in the Cape Colony Parliament, but he has never considered it worth the time to deny the report. His political success depends in no little measure upon his personal acquaintanceship with the small men of his party, and his method of treating them with as much consideration and respect as those who have greater influence. He is in constant communication with the leaders of the rural communities, and misses no opportunity to show his appreciation of their support. Mr. Rhodes may be kingly when he is among kings, but he is also a farmer among farmers, and among the Cape Dutch and Boers such a metamorphosis is the necessary stepping-stone to the hearts and votes of that numerous people. It is not uncommon to find Mr. Rhodes among a party of farmers or transport riders each one of whom has better clothing than the multimillionaire.

When he was in the Cape Parliament Mr. Rhodes wore a hat which was so shabby that it became the subject of newspaper importance. When he is in Rhodesia he dons the oldest suit of clothing in his wardrobe, and follows the habits of the pioneers who are settling the country. He sleeps in a native kraal when he is not near a town, and eats of the same canned beef and crackers that his Chartered Company serves to its mounted police. When he is in that primeval country he despises ostentation and displays in his honour, and will travel fifty miles on horseback in an opposite direction in order to avoid a formal proceeding of any nature. Two years ago, when the railroad to Buluwayo, the capital of Rhodesia, was formally opened, Mr. Rhodes telegraphed his regrets, and intimated that he was ill. As a matter of fact he travelled night and day in order to escape to a place where telegrams and messages could not reach him. When his host suggested that he was missing many entertainments and the society of the most distinguished men of South Africa, Mr. Rhodes smiled and said: " For that reason I escaped."

Formality bores him, and he would rather live a month coatless and collarless in a native kraal with an old colony story-teller than spend half an hour at a state dinner in the governor's mansion. It is related in this connection that Mr. Rhodes was one of a distinguished party who attended the opening of a railroad extension near Cape Town. While the speeches were being made, and the chairman was trying to find him, Mr. Rhodes slipped quietly away, and was discovered discarding his clothing preparatory to enjoying a bath in a near-by creek.

Mr. Rhodes is unmarried, and throughout the country has the reputation of being an avowed hater of women. He believes that a woman is an impediment to a man's existence until he has attained the object and aim of his life, and has become deserving of luxuries. He not only believes in that himself, but takes advantage of every opportunity to impress the belief upon the minds of those around him. In the summer of 1897 a captain in the volunteer army, and one of his most faithful lieutenants in Mashonaland, asked Mr. Rhodes for a three months' leave of absence to go to Cape Colony. The captain had been through many native campaigns, and richly deserved a vacation, although that was not the real object of his request for leave. The man wanted to go to Cape Colony to marry, and by severe cross-examination Mr. Rhodes learned that such was the case.

"I can not let you go to Cape Colony; I want you to start for London to-morrow. I'll cable instructions when you arrive there," said Mr. Rhodes, and the wedding was postponed. When the captain reached London, a cablegram from Mr. Rhodes said simply, "Study London for three months."

Nowhere in South Africa is there anything more interesting than Groote Schuur, the country residence of Mr. Rhodes, at Rondebosch, a suburb of Cape Town. He has found time amid his momentous public duties to make his estate the most magnificent on the continent of Africa. Besides a mansion which is a relic of the first settlers of the peninsula, and now a palace worthy of a king's occupancy, there is an estate which consists of hundreds of acres of land overlooking both the Atlantic and Indian Oceans, and under the walls of Table Mountain, the curio of a country. In addition to this, there are a zoölogical collection, which comprises almost every specimen of African fauna that will thrive in captivity, and hundreds of flowering trees and plants brought from great distances to enrich the beauty of the landscape.

The estate, which comprises almost twelve hundred acres, is situated about five miles to the north of Cape Town, on the narrowest part of the peninsula, through which the waters of the two oceans seem ever anxious to rush and clasp hands. It lies along the northwestern base of Table Mountain, and stretches down toward the waters of Table Bay and northward toward the death-dealing desert known as the Great Karroo. From one of the shady streets winding toward Cape Town there stretches a fine avenue of lofty pines and oaks to the mansion of Groote Schuur, which, as its name indicates, was originally a granary, where two hundred years ago the Dutch colonizers hoarded their stores of grain and guarded them against the attacks of thieving natives.

Although many changes have been made in the structure since it was secured by Mr. Rhodes, it still preserves the quaint architectural characteristics of Holland. The scrolled gables, moulded chimney pots, and wide verandas, or "stoeps," are none the less indicative of the tendencies of the old settlers than the Dutch cabinets, bureaus, and other household furniture that still remains in the mansion from those early days.

The entire estate breathes of the old Dutch era. Everything has the ancient setting, although not at the expense of modern convenience. While the buildings and grounds are arranged in the picturesque style of Holland, the furnishings and comforts are the most modern that the countries of Europe afford. The library contains, besides such classics as a graduate of Oxford would have, one of the largest collections of books and manuscripts bearing on Africa in existence. In the same room is a museum of souvenirs connected with Mr. Rhodes's work of extending English empire toward the heart of the continent. There are flags captured in wars with the Portuguese, Union Jacks riddled with shot and cut by assegai, and hundreds of curiosities gathered in Rhodesia after the conquest of the natives. In this building have gathered for conference the men who laid the foundations for all the great enterprises of South Africa. There the Jameson raid was planned, it is said, and there, the Boers say, the directors of the British South Africa Chartered Company were drinking champagne while the forces of Dr. Jameson were engaged in mortal combat with those of Kruger near Johannesburg.

Surrounding the mansion are most beautiful gardens, such as can be found only in semitropical climates. In the foreground of the view from the back part of the house is a Dutch garden, rising in three terraces from the marble-paved courtyard to a grassy knoll, fringed with tall pines, and dotted here and there with graves of former dwellers at Groote Schuur.

Behind the pine fringe, but only at intervals obscured by it, is the background of the picture—the bush-clad slopes of Table Mountain and the Devil's Peak, near enough for every detail of their strange formations and innumerable attractions to be observed. Art and Nature have joined hands everywhere to make lovely landscapes, in which the colour effects are produced by hydrangeas, azaleas, and scores of other flowers, growing in the utmost profusion. Besides the mimosa, palms, firs, and other tropical trees that add beauty to the grounds, there is a low tree which is found nowhere else on earth. Its leaves are like the purest silver, and form a charming contrast to the deep green of the firs and the vivid brightness of the flowers that are everywhere around.

Undoubtedly, however, the most interesting feature of the estate is the natural zoölogical garden. It is quite unique to have in this immense park, with drives six miles in length and ornamentations brought thousands of miles, wild animals of every variety wandering about with as much freedom as if they were in their native haunts. In this collection are represented every kind of African deer and antelope. Zebra, kangaroo, giraffe, emu, pheasant, and ostrich seem to be perfectly contented with their adopted home, and have become so tame that the presence of human beings has no terrors for them.

This vast estate, which cost Mr. Rhodes several million dollars to bring to its present condition, sees but little of the former Premier of Cape Colony. His vast enterprises in the diamond fields of Kimberley and in the new country which bears his name require so much of his time that he but seldom visits it. But his inability to enjoy the product of his brain and labour does not cause the estate to be unappreciated, for he has thrown this unique and charming pleasure resort open to the public, and by them it is regarded as a national possession.

CHAPTER VIII

THE BOER GOVERNMENT—CIVIL AND MILITARY

THE Constitution, or Grondwet, of the South African Republic is a modified counterpart of that of the United States. It differs in some salient features, but in its entirety it has the same general foundation and the same objects. The executive head of the Government is the President, who is elected for a term of five years. He directs the policy of the Government, suggests the trend of the laws, and oversees the conduct of the Executive Council, which constitutes the real Government. The Executive Council consists of three heads of departments and six unofficial members of the First Raad. These nine officials are the authors of all laws, treaties, and policies that are proposed to the Volksraads, which constitute the third part of the Government. There are two Volksraads, one similar in purpose to our Senate, and the other, the second Volksraad, not unlike our House of Representatives, but with far less power.

The first Volksraad consists of twenty-seven members elected from and by the burghers, or voters, who were born in the country. A naturalized burgher is ineligible to the upper House. The twenty-seven members of the Second Raad are naturalized burghers, and are voted for only by men who have received the franchise. The second House has control of the management of the Government works, telephones, mails, and mines, and has but little voice in the real government of the country. Its members are undoubtedly more progressive and have more modern ideas than those of the First Raad, and introduce many bills which would be of undoubted benefit to the country, but the upper House invariably vetoes all bills that reach them from that Raad. The First Raad receives bills and suggestions from the Executive Council or from the President himself, but refers them to a commission for investigation before any action is taken upon them. The evidence in support of proposed measures does not reach the Raad, which only concerns itself with the report of the commission. The Raad can, by motion, make a suggestion to the Executive Council that a certain measure should be formulated, but the Executive Council and the President have the authority to ignore the suggestion, leaving the First Raad without a vestige of authority. The upper House concerns itself chiefly with the questions of finance, changes in the Constitution, and the care of the natives. As the question of finance is so closely connected with almost every subject that comes before the Government, it follows that the First Raad concerns itself with practically the entire business of the Government. The popular conception is that the Second Raad, being composed of naturalized citizens, takes less interest in the affairs of the country, and can therefore be less safely trusted with their conduct than the old burghers and Voortrekkers of the upper House, who would rather declare war against a foreign power than pass a law in the least unfavourable to their own country's interests. In consequence of the Second Raad's infinitesimal powers, almost the entire lawmaking power of the Government is vested in the Executive Council and the First Raad.

The First Raad of the Transvaal Republic is the direct successor of the democratic form of government that was established by the Voortrekkers of 1835 when they were journeying from Cape Colony to the northern lands. The Second Raad was established in 1890, in order that the Uitlanders might have representation in the government of the country. It was believed that the newly arrived population would take advantage of the opportunities thus offered to take part in the legislation of the republic, and in that way bridge over the gulf which had been formed between the two races. The Uitlanders cared little for the privilege offered to them, and so far in the history of the Second Raad less than half a score of its members have been elected by the new population.

The annual sessions of the Volksraads commence on the first Monday in May, and continue until all the business of the republic has been transacted. The members of the two

Houses receive fifteen dollars a day, and seventy-five cents an hour for services extending over more than the five hours a day required by the law. The chairmen, or voorzitters, of the Raads receive seventeen dollars and fifty cents a day, and one dollar an hour for extra time.

The sessions of the Raad are held in the new million-dollar Government House in the central part of the town of Pretoria, and are open to the public except when executive business is being transacted. The Raad chambers are exquisitely fitted out with rich furniture and tapestries, the windows are of costly stained glass, and the walls lavishly decorated with carved wood and fine paintings of the country's notable men. On a lofty elevation facing the entrance to the First Raad chamber is a heavily carved mahogany desk, behind which is seated the chairman. On his right is a seat for the President, while on the right side of that are the nine chairs for the Executive Council. Directly in front and beneath the chairman's desk are the desks of the three official secretaries, and in front of these, in semicircular form, the two rows of seats and desks of the Raad members. In the rear of the chamber on either side of the entrance are chairs for visitors, while high in the left side of the lofty chamber is a small balcony for the newspaper men.

All the members of the Raad are obliged by law to wear black clothing and white neckties. This law was framed to prevent some of the rural members from appearing in their burgher costumes, and has had the effect of making of the Boer Raads a most sombre-looking body of lawmakers. Almost all members wear long frock-coats, silk hats, and heavy black boots, and when, during the recesses, they appear on the piazza of the Government Building with huge pipes in their mouths, the wisdom of the black-clothing law is not apparent. There is little formality in the proceedings of the Raads. Certain rules are necessarily followed, but the members attack a bill in much the same vehement manner as they would a lion or a panther. There is little eloquence in the taal, or dialect, that is spoken in the Raads, and the similes and metaphors bespeak the open veldt and the transport path rather than the council chamber of a nation.

The black-garbed legislators make no pretensions to dignified procedure, and when a playful member trips another so that he falls to the floor, or pelts him with paper balls, the whole Raad joins in laughter. The gaudily dressed pages—one of them is sixty-five years old and wears a long beard—are on terms of great familiarity with the members, and have become mildly famous throughout the country on account of some practical jokes they have perpetrated upon the members. It is only justice to say that these light proceedings take place only when the President is not present. When he arrives in the chamber every one rises and remains standing until the President has seated himself. He generally takes a deep interest in the subjects before the House, and not infrequently speaks at length upon measures for which he desires a certain line of action. Many of President Kruger's most important speeches have been delivered to the Raads, and so great is his influence over the members that his wishes are rarely disregarded. When he meets with opposition to his views he quickly loses his temper, and upon one occasion called a certain member who opposed him a traitor, and angrily left the chamber. A short time afterward he returned and apologized to the member and to the Raad for having in his anger used unseemly language.

One of the most disappointing scenes to be observed in Pretoria is the horde of Uitlander politicians and speculators who are constantly besieging the Raad members and the Government officials. At probably no other national capital are the legislators tempted to such a great extent as are the Boers, who, for the most part, are ignorant of the ways of the world and unfamiliar with great amounts of money. Every train from Johannesburg, the Uitlander capital, takes to Pretoria scores of lobbyists, who use all their powers, both of persuasion and finance, to influence the minds of the legislators, either in the way of granting valuable concessions for small considerations or of securing the passage of bills favourable to the lobbyists. It is no wonder that the

Uitlanders declare that less than one fourth of the Raad members are unassailably honest and that all the others can be bribed. The Boer alone is not blameworthy who, having never possessed more than one hundred dollars at one time, yields to the constant importunities of the lobbyist and sells his vote for several thousand dollars.

Beset by such influences, the Raad members are naturally suspicious of every bill that is brought before them for consideration. Their deliberations are marked by a feeling of insecurity akin to that displayed by the inhabitants of a sheep-pen surrounded by a pack of hungry wolves. They fear to make a move in any direction lest their motives be misunderstood, or they play into the hands of the Uitlanders. As a consequence of this external pressure, progress in the improvement of the methods of governing the country has been slow. One of the results of the Volksraad's fearfulness is the absence of local governments throughout the republic. There are no municipalities, counties, or townships which can formulate and execute local laws. Even Johannesburg, a city of one hundred thousand population, has no municipal government, although several attempts have been made to establish one.

The Raads are burdened with the necessity of attending to all the details which govern the administration of every city, village, hamlet, and district in the entire country, and the time consumed in doing all this leaves little for the weightier affairs of state. If a five-dollar road bridge is required in an out-of-the-way place in the northern part of the republic, the Raad is obliged to discuss the matter. If an application for a liquor license comes from a distant point in the interior, the Raad is compelled to investigate its character before it can be voted upon. The disadvantages of this system are so evident that it is hardly conceivable that no remedy has been applied long ago, but the fear of local mismanagement has prevented the Raad from ridding itself of this encumbrance upon its time and patience.

Every legislature of whatever country has its idiosyncracies, and the Raad is no exception. Laws are upon the statute books of some of the American States that are quite as remarkable as some of those made by the Boer legislators. Bills quite as marvellous have been introduced and defeated in the legislatures of all countries. The Boer Volksraad has no monopoly of men with quaint ideas. The examples of Raad workmanship here given are rare, but true nevertheless:

A man named Dums, whose big farm on the border became British territory through a treaty, sued the Transvaal Government for damages, whereupon the Raad passed a law that Dums could never sue the Government for anything. The High Court sustained the law, and Dums is now a poor cab-driver in Pretoria. Another man sued the Government for damages for injuries resulting from a fall in the street. He was successful in his suit, but the Raad immediately thereafter passed a law making it impossible for any person to sue the Government for injuries received on public property.

During a severe drought in the Transvaal an American professional rain-maker asked the

Raad for a concession allowing him the exclusive privilege to precipitate rain by means of explosives in the air. The Raad had a long and animated discussion on the subject, owing to the opposition of several of the less enlightened members, who declared that the project was sacrilegious. "It is a sin," they declared, "to poke your fingers in the Lord's eye to make him weep." The abiding faith which some of the Raad members have in divine guidance is illustrated by a discussion that took place in the body shortly after the Jameson raid. One member declared that "the Lord will assist us in this matter if we will only bide our time," whereupon another member rose and said, "If we do not soon get down to business and do something without the Lord's assistance, the Lord will take a holiday and let the Transvaal go to hell." A law which was in effect for almost two years made it a misdemeanour for any one to sing "God save the Queen" or "Rule Britannia" in the country. Mass meetings are prohibited in the Transvaal, but Germany and other countries with less political foment have equally stringent regulations on the same subject, so the Uitlanders' grievance on that account is nullified.

Second to that of the Volksraad, the highest power in the Government of the country is the High Court, which is composed of some of the ablest jurists in South Africa. From a constitutional standpoint the High Court has no right or power to review the acts of the Volksraad. The Constitution of the country gives supreme power to the Volksraad in all legislative matters, and when a chief justice of the High Court recently attempted to extend his jurisdiction over the acts of the Volksraad that body unceremoniously dismissed him. The purpose of that part of the Constitution which relates to the subjugation of the High Court is to prevent some influential enemy of the republic from debauching the High Court and in that way defying the authority of the Volksraad. In a country which has so many peculiar conditions and circumstances to contend with, the safety of its institutions depends upon the centralization of its legislative and administrative branches, and the wisdom of the early burghers who framed the Constitution so that the entire governing power lay in the hands of the country's real patriots has been amply demonstrated upon several occasions.

The civil and criminal laws of the country are administered throughout the different political divisions by local magistrates, called land-drosts, who also collect the revenues of the district and inform the Volksraad of the needs of the people under their jurisdiction. The land-drost is the prototype of the old-time American country squire, in that he settles disputes, awards damages, and conducts official business generally. In the majority of cases the land-drosts are aged persons who have the respect and esteem of the members of the community in which they dwell and to whom they bear the relation of fatherly advisers in all things. In Johannesburg and Pretoria the land-drosts are men of eminent station in the legal profession of South Africa, and are drawn from all parts of the country, regardless of their political or racial qualifications. All the court proceedings are conducted in the Dutch language, and none but Dutch-speaking lawyers are admitted to practise before the bar. The law of the land is Holland-Roman.

The military branch of the Government is undoubtedly the best and most effective because it is the simplest. It is almost primitive in its simplicity, yet for effectiveness its superior is not easily found. The Transvaal glories in its army, and, as every man between the ages of sixteen and sixty is a nominal member of the army, nothing is left undone to make it worthy of its glory. The standing army of the republic numbers less than two hundred men, and these are not always actively engaged. A detachment of about twenty soldiers is generally on duty in the vicinity of the Government House at Pretoria, and the others are stationed at the different forts throughout the republic. The real army of the Transvaal, however, is composed of the volunteer soldiers, who can be mobilized with remarkable facility.

The head of the army is the commandant-general, who has his headquarters in Pretoria.

He is under the immediate jurisdiction of the Volksraad and the President, who have the power to declare war and direct its conduct. Second in authority to the commandant-general are the commandants, permanent officials who have charge of the military affairs of the seventeen districts of the republic. Under the old South African burgher law each commandant in any emergency " commandeers " a certain portion of men from his district.

The various districts are subdivided into divisions in charge of field-cornets and assistant field-cornets. As soon as the commandant-general issues an order for the mobilization of the volunteer army the commandants and their assistants, the field-cornets, speedily go from one house to another in their districts and summon the burghers from their homes. When the burgher receives the call, he provides his own gun, horse, and forage, and hastens to the district rendezvous, where he places himself under the orders of the field-cornet. After all the burghers of the district have gathered together, the body proceeds into an adjoining district, where it

THE BOER GOVERNMENT 207

joins the forces that have been similarly mobilized there. As a certain number of districts are obliged to join their forces at a defined locality, the forces of the republic are consequently divided into different army divisions under the supervisions of the commandants.

In the event that Pretoria were threatened with attack, the order would be given to move all the forces to that city. The districts on the border would gather their men and march toward Pretoria, carrying with them all the forces of the districts through which they were obliged to pass. So simple and perfect is the system that within forty-eight hours after the call is issued by the commandant-general four army divisions, representing the districts in the four quarters of the republic and consisting of all the able-bodied men in the country, can be mobilized on the outskirts of Pretoria. It is doubtful whether there is another nation on earth that can gather its entire fighting strength at its seat of government in such a brief time.

The Transvaal Boer is constantly prepared for the call to arms. He has his own rifle and ammunition at his home, and when the call comes he need only bridle his horse—if he is so fortunate as to possess an animal so rare in the Transvaal—stuff several pounds of biltong, or dried beef, in his pockets, and commence the march over the veldt to the district rendezvous. He can depend upon his wife and children to care for the flocks and herds; but if the impending danger appears to be great, the cattle are deserted and the women and children are taken to a rendezvous specially planned for such an emergency. If there is a need, the Boer woman will stand side by side with her husband or her brother or her sweetheart, and will allow no one to surpass her in repelling the attacks of the enemy. Joan of Arcs have been as numerous in the Boer armies as they have been unheralded.

The head of the military branch of the Transvaal Government for many years has been Commandant-General P. J. Joubert, who, following President Kruger, is the ablest as well as the most popular Boer in South Africa. General Joubert is the best type of the Boer fighter in the country, and as he represents the army, he has always been a favourite with the class which would rather decide a disputed point by means of the rifle than by diplomacy, as practised by President Kruger. General Joubert, although the head of the army, is not of a quarrelsome disposition, and he too believes in the peaceful arbitration of differences rather than a resort to arms. By the Uitlanders he is considered to be the most liberal Boer in the republic, and he has upon numerous occasions shown that he would treat the newcomers in the country with more leniency than the Kruger Government if he were in power.

In his capacity of Vice-President of the republic he has been as impotent as the Vice-President is in the United States, but his influence has always been wielded with a view of harmonizing the differences of the native and alien populations. Twice the more liberal and progressive party of the Boers has put him forward as a candidate for the presidency in opposition to Mr. Kruger, and each time he has been defeated by only a small majority. The younger Boers who have come in touch with the more modern civilization have steadfastly supported General Joubert, while the older Boers, who are ever fearful that any one but Mr. Kruger would grant too many concessions to the Uitlanders, have wielded their influence against him. Concerning the franchise for Uitlanders, General Joubert is more liberal than President Kruger, who holds that the stability of the Government depends upon the exclusiveness of the franchise privilege. General Joubert believes that there are many persons among the Uitlanders who have a real desire to become citizens of the republic and to take part in the government. He believes that an intending burgher should take an oath of fidelity, and afterward be prepared to do what he can for the country, either in peace or war. If after three or four years the applicant for the franchise has shown that he worked in the interests of the country and obeyed its laws, General Joubert believes that the Uitlander should enjoy all the privileges that a native burgher enjoys—namely, voting for the candidates for the presidency and the First Volksraad.

General Joubert's name has been connected with Transvaal history almost as long and as prominently as that of President Kruger. The two men are virtually the fathers of the Boer republic. General Joubert has always been the man who fought the battles with armies, while Mr. Kruger conducted the diplomatic battles, and both were equally successful in their parts. General Joubert, as a youth among the early trekkers from Natal, was reared amid warfare. During the Transvaal's early battles with the natives he was a volunteer soldier under the then Commandant-General Kruger, and later, when the war of independence was fought, he became General Joubert. He commanded the forces which fought the battles of Laing's Nek, Bronkhorst Spruit, and Majuba Hill, and he was one of the triumvirate that conducted the affairs of the Government during that crucial time. He has been Vice-President of the republic since the independence of the country has been re-established, and conducted the affairs of the army during the time when Jameson's troopers threatened the safety of the country. He has had a notable career in the service of his country, and as a reward for his services he is deserving of nothing less than the presidency of the republic after Mr. Kruger's life-work is ended.

General Joubert is no less distinguished as a diplomatist among his countrymen than President Kruger, and many stories are current in Pretoria showing that he has been able to accomplish many things wherein Mr. Kruger failed. An incident which occurred immediately after the Jameson raid, and which is repeated here exactly as related by one of the participants of the affair, is illustrative of General Joubert and his methods of dealing with his own people. The story is given in almost the exact language of the narrator who was the eyewitness:

"Shortly after Jameson and his officers were brought to Pretoria, President Kruger called about twenty of the Boer commanders to his house for a consultation. The townspeople were highly excited, and the presence of the men who had tried to destroy the republic aggravated their condition so that there were few calm minds in the capital. President

THE BOER GOVERNMENT

Kruger was deeply affected by the seriousness of the events of the days before, but counselled all those present to be calm. There were some in the gathering who advised that Jameson and his men should be shot immediately, while one man jocosely remarked that they should not be treated so leniently, and suggested that a way to make them suffer would be to cut off their ears.

"One of the men who was obliged to leave the meeting gave this account to the waiting throngs in the street, and a few hours afterward the cable had carried the news to Europe and America, with the result that the Boers were called brutal and inhuman. President Kruger used all his influence and eloquence to save the lives of the prisoners, and for a long time he was unsuccessful in securing the smallest amount of sympathy for Jameson and his men. It was dawn when General Joubert was won to the President's way of thinking, and he continued the argument in behalf of the prisoners.

"'My friends, I will ask you to listen patiently to me for several minutes,' he commenced. 'I will tell you the story of the farmer and the neighbour's dog. Suppose that near your farm lives a man whose valuable dogs attack your sheep and kill many. Will you shoot the dogs as soon as you see them, and in that way make yourself liable for damages greater than the value of the sheep that were destroyed? Or will you catch the dogs when you are able to do so and, carrying them to your neighbour, say to him: "I have caught your dogs; now pay me for the damage they have done me, and they shall be returned to you."'

"After a moment's silence General Joubert's face lighted up joyfully, and he exclaimed:

"'We have the neighbour's dogs in the jail. What shall we do with them?'

"The parable was effective, and the council of war decided almost instantly to deliver the prisoners to the British Government."

CHAPTER IX

CAUSES OF THE PRESENT DISSENSIONS

THE politicians and the speculators have been the bane of South Africa. Ill-informed secretaries of the British Colonial Office might augment the list, but their stupidity in treating with colonial grievances is so proverbial as to admit them to the rank of natural or providential causes of dissension. Until the Boer Government came into the foreground, the politicians and speculators used South Africa as a huge chessboard, whereon they could manipulate the political and commercial affairs of hundreds of thousands of persons to suit their own fancies and convenience.

It was a *dilettante* politician who operated in South Africa and could not make a cat's-paw of the colonial secretary in Downing Street, and it was a stupid speculator who was unable to be the power behind the enthroned politician. And South Africa has been the victim. Hundreds of men have gone to South Africa and have become millionaires, but thousands remain in the country praying for money wherewith to return home. The former are the politicians and the speculators; the latter are the miners, the workingmen, and the tradespeople.

It is a country where the man with a million becomes a multimillionaire, and the man with hundreds becomes penniless. It is the wealthy man's footstool and the poor man's cemetery. Men go there to acquire riches; few go there to assist in making it tenable for white men. Thousands go there with the avowed intention of making their fortunes and then to return. Those who go there as came the immigrants to America—to settle and develop the new country—can be counted only by the score. Of the million white people south of the Zambezi, probably one half are mere fortune-seekers, who would leave the country the very instant they secured a moderate fortune.

These have the welfare of the country at heart only in so far as it interferes or assists them in attaining their desired goal. They

CAUSES OF THE PRESENT DISSENSIONS 217

would ask that Portugal be allowed to rule all of South Africa if they received the assurance that the much-sought-after fortune could be secured six months sooner. They have no conscience other than that which prevents them from stabbing a man to relieve him of his money. They go to the gold and diamond fields to secure wealth, and not to assist in developing law and order, good government, or good institutions.

The other half of the white population is composed of men and women who were born in the country — Afrikanders, Dutch, Boers, and other racial representatives, and others who have emigrated thither from the densely populated countries of Europe, with the intention of remaining in the country and taking part in its government and institutions. These classes comprise the South Africans, who love their country and take a real interest in its development and progress. They know its needs and prospects, and are abundantly able to conduct its government so that it will benefit Boer, Englishman, Dutchman, Natalian, and native.

The defects in the Government of Cape Colony and Natal are the natural results of the handicaps that have been placed on the local legislation by the Colonial Office in London, who are as ignorant of the real conditions of their colonies as a Zulu chieftain is of the political situation in England. The colonial papers teem with letters from residents who express their indignation at the methods employed by the Colonial Office in dealing with colonial affairs. Especially is this the case in Natal, the Eden of South Africa, where the dealings of the Colonial Office with regard to the Zulus have been stupidly carried on. South African men of affairs who are not bigoted do not hesitate to express their opinion that Cape Colony and Natal have been retarded a quarter of a century in their natural growth by the handicap of the Colonial Office. Their opinion is based upon the fact that every war, with the exception of several native outbreaks, has been caused by blundering in the Colonial Office, and that all the wars have retarded the natural growth and development of the colonies to an aggregate of twenty-five years. In this estimate is not included the great harm

Cape Colony Government House, at Cape Town.

CAUSES OF THE PRESENT DISSENSIONS

to industries that has been caused by the score or more of heavy war clouds with which the country has been darkened during the last half century. These being some of the difficulties with which the two British colonies in South Africa are beset, it can be readily inferred to what extent the Boers of the Transvaal have had cause for grievance. In their dealings with the Boers the British have invariably assumed the rôle of aristocrats, and have looked upon and treated the "trekkers" as *sans-culottes*.

This natural antipathy of one race for another has given glorious opportunities for strife, and neither one nor the other has ever failed to take quick advantage. The struggle between the Boers and the British began in Cape Colony almost one hundred years ago, and it has continued, with varying degrees of bitterness, until the present day. The recent disturbances in the Transvaal affairs date from the conclusion of the war of independence in 1881. When the Peace Commissioners met there was inserted in the treaty one small clause which gave to England her only right to interfere in the political affairs of the Transvaal.

The Boer country at that time was considered of such little worth that Gladstone declared it was not of sufficient value to be honoured with a place under the British flag. To the vast majority of the British people it was a matter of indifference whether the Transvaal was an independent country or a dependency of their own Government. The clause which was allowed to enter the treaty unnoticed, and which during recent years has figured so prominently in the discussions of South African affairs, reads:

"The South African Republic will conclude no treaty or engagement with any state or nation other than the Orange Free State, nor with any native tribe to the eastward or the westward of the republic, until the same has been approved by her Majesty the Queen. Such approval shall be considered to have been granted if her Majesty's Government shall not, within six months after receiving a copy of such treaty (which shall be delivered to them immediately upon its completion), have notified that the conclusion of the treaty is in conflict with the interests of Great Britain, or of

CAUSES OF THE PRESENT DISSENSIONS

any of her Majesty's possessions in South Africa."

When the contents of the treaty were published to the Boer people, many of them objected strongly to this clause, and insisted that it gave the British too great power in the affairs of the republic, and a strenuous effort was made to have the offending clause eliminated. In the year 1883 a deputation, which included Paul Kruger, was sent to London, with a view of obtaining the abolition of the suzerainty. This deputation negotiated a new convention the following year, from which the word "suzerainty" and the stipulations in regard thereto were removed. In their report to the Volksraad, made in 1884, the deputation stated that the new convention put an end to the British suzerainty.

February 4, 1884, in a letter to Lord Derby, then in charge of British affairs, the deputation announced to him that they expected an agreement to be contained in the treaty relative to the abolition of the suzerainty. In his reply of a week later, Lord Derby made a statement upon which the Boers base their strongest claim that the suzerainty was abolished. He said:

"By the omission of those articles of the convention of Pretoria which assigned to her Majesty and to the British resident certain specific powers and functions connected with the internal government and the foreign relations of the Transvaal state, your Government will be left free to govern the country without interference, and to conduct its diplomatic intercourse and shape its foreign policy, subject only to the requirement embodied in the fourth article of the new draft, that any treaty with a foreign state shall not have effect without the approval of the Queen."

For a period of almost ten years the suzerainty of England over the Transvaal was an unknown quantity. With the exception of several Government officials, there were hardly any Englishmen in the country, and no one had the slightest interest in the affairs of the Transvaal Government. When gold was discovered in the Randt in quantities that equalled those of the early days of the California gold fields, an unparalleled influx of Englishmen and

CAUSES OF THE PRESENT DISSENSIONS 223

foreigners followed, and in several years the city of Johannesburg had sprung up in the veldt.

The opening of hundreds of mines, and the consequent increase in expenditures, made it necessary for the Transvaal Government to increase its revenues. Mining laws had to be formulated, new offices had to be created, hundreds of new officials had to be appointed, and all this required the expenditure of more money in one year than the Government had spent in a decade before the opening of the mines. The Government found itself in a quandary, and it solved the problem of finances as many a stronger and wealthier government has done.

Concessions were granted to dynamite, railway, electric light, electric railway, water, and many other companies, and these furnished to the Government the nucleus upon which depended its financial existence. Few of the concessions were obtained by British subjects, and when the monopolies took advantage of their opportunities, and raised the price of dynamite and the rates for carrying freight, the Englishmen, who owned all the mines, naturally objected. The Boer Government, having bound itself hand and foot when hard pressed for money, was unable to compel the concessionaries to reduce their rates.

At that period of the Randt's existence the speculators appeared, and soon thereafter the London Stock Exchange became a factor in the affairs of the Randt. Where the Stock Exchange leads, the politicians follow, and they too soon became interested in South African affairs. Then the treaty of 1883 was found in the Colonial Office archives, and next appears a demand to the Boer Government that all British residents of the Transvaal be allowed to vote. The Boers refused to give the franchise to any applicant unless he first renounced his allegiance to other countries, and, as the British subjects declined to accede to the request, the politicians became busily engaged in formulating other plans whereby England might obtain control of the country.

At that inopportune time Jameson's troopers entered the Transvaal territory and attempted to take forcible possession of the country; but they were unsuccessful, and only succeeded in directing the world's sympathy to the Boers. The Jameson raid was practically Cecil J. Rhodes's first important attempt to add the Transvaal to the list of South African additions he has made to the British Empire. The result was especially galling to him, as it was the first time his great political schemes failed of success.

But Rhodes is not the man to weep over disasters. Before the excitement over the raid had subsided, Rhodes had concocted a plan to inflict a commercial death upon the Transvaal, and in that manner force it to beg for the protection of the English flag. He opened Rhodesia, an adjoining country, for settlement, and by glorifying the country, its mineral and agricultural wealth, and by offering golden inducements to Transvaal tradespeople, miners, and even Transvaal subjects, he hoped to cause such an efflux from the Transvaal that the Government would be embarrassed in less than two years. The country which bears his name was found to be amazingly free from mountains of gold and rivers of honey, and the several thousand persons who had faith in his alluring promises remained in Rhodesia less than a year, and then returned to the Transvaal.

The reports of the Rhodesian country that were brought back by the disappointed miners and settlers were not flattering to the condition of the country or the justice of the Government. Of two evils, they chose the lesser, and again placed themselves under the Kruger Government. When revolution and enticement failed to bring the Transvaal under the British flag, Rhodes inaugurated a political propaganda. His last resort was the Colonial Office in London, and in that alone lay the only course by which he could attain his object.

Again the franchise question was resorted to as the ground of the contention, the dynamite and railway subjects having been so thoroughly debated as to be as void of ground for further contention as they had always been foreign to British control or interference. The question of granting the right of voting to the Uitlanders in the Transvaal is one which so vitally affects the future life of the Government that the Boers' concession of that right would be tantamount to presenting the country to the British Government.

Ninety-nine per cent. of the Uitlanders of the Transvaal are no more than transient citizens. They were attracted thither by the gold mines and the attendant industries, and they have no thought of staying in the Transvaal a minute after they have amassed a fortune or a competency. Under no consideration would they remain in the country for the rest of their lives, because the climate and nature of the country are not conducive to a desire for long residence. It has been demonstrated that less than one per cent. of the Uitlanders had sufficient interest in the country to pass through the formality of securing naturalization papers preparatory to becoming eligible for the franchise.

The Boer Government has offered that all Uitlanders of nine years' residence, having certain unimportant qualifications, should be enfranchised in two years, and that others should be enfranchised in seven years—two years for naturalization and five more years' resident—before acquiring the right to vote.

There is a provision for a property qualification, which makes it necessary for the naturalized citizen to own a house of no less value than two hundred and fifty dollars in renting value, or an income of one thousand dollars. The residence clause in the Transvaal qualifications compares favourably with those of London, where an Englishman from any part of the country and settling in the municipality is obliged to live two years and have certain property qualifications before acquiring the right of franchise.

In full knowledge of these conditions the Uitlanders insist upon having an unconditional franchise—one that will require nothing more than a two-years' residence in the country. The Boers are well aware of the results that would follow the granting of the concessions demanded, but not better so than the Uitlanders who make the demands. The latest Transvaal statistics place the number of Boer burghers in the country at less than thirty thousand. At the lowest estimate there are in the Transvaal fifty thousand Uitlanders having the required qualifications, and all of these would become voters in two years. At the first election held after the two years had elapsed the Uitlanders would be victorious, and those whom they elected would control the machinery of the Government. The Uitlanders' plan is as transparent as air, yet it has the approval and sanction of the English politicians, press, and public.

The propaganda which Rhodes and other politicians and stock brokers interested in the Transvaal gold mines inaugurated a short time after the Jameson raid has been successful in arousing the people in England to what they have been led to believe is a situation unequalled in the history of the empire-building. But there is a parallel case. At the same time the British Parliament was discussing the subject of the alleged injustice under which the English residents of the Transvaal were suffering, the colonial secretary was engaged in disposing of grievances which reached him from the Dutch residents of British Guiana, in South America, and which recited conditions parallel to those complained of by the Uitlanders. The grievances were made by foreign residents of English territory, instead of by English subjects in a foreign country, and consequently demanded less serious attention, but their justice was none the less patent. The three thousand native Dutch voters in British Guiana have no voice in the legislative or administrative branches of the colonial government, owing to the peculiar laws which give to the three thousand British-born citizens the complete control of the franchise. The population of the colony is three hundred thousand, yet the three thousand British subjects make and administer the laws for the other two hundred and ninety-seven thousand inhabitants, who compose the mining and agricultural communities and are treated with the same British contempt as the Boers. The Dutch residents have made many appeals for a fuller representation in the Government, but no reforms have been inaugurated or promised.

The few grievances which the Uitlanders had before the Jameson raid have been multiplied a hundredfold and no epithet is too venomous for them to apply to the Boers. The letters in the home newspapers have allied the name of the Boers with every vilifying adjective in the English dictionary, and returning politicians have never failed to supply the others that do not appear in the book.

Petitions with thousands of names, some real, but many non-existent, have been forwarded to the Colonial Office and to every other office in London where they would be received, and these have recited grievances that even the patient Boer Volksraad had never heard about. It has been a propaganda of petitions and letters the like of which has no parallel in the history of politics. It has been successful in arousing sentiment favourable to the Uitlanders, and at this time there is hardly a handful of persons in England who are not willing to testify to the utter degradation of the Boers.

Another branch of the propaganda operated through the Stock Exchange, and its results were probably more practical than those of the literary branch. It is easier to reach the English masses through the Stock Exchange than by any other means. Whenever one of the " Kaffir " or Transvaal companies failed to make both ends meet in a manner which pleased the stockholders, it was only necessary to blame the Boer Government for having impeded the digging of gold, and the stockholders promptly outlined to the Colonial Office the policy it should pursue toward the Boers.

The impressions that are formed in watching the tide of events in the Transvaal are that the Boer Government is not greatly inferior to the Government of Lord Salisbury and Secretary Chamberlain. The only appreciable difference between the two is that the Boers are fighting the cause of the masses against the classes, while the English are fighting that of the classes against the masses. In England, where the rich have the power, the poor pay the taxes, while in the Transvaal the poor have the power and compel the rich to pay the taxes. If the Transvaal taxes were of such serious proportions as to be almost unbearable, there might be a cause for interference by the Uitlander capitalists who own the mines, but there no injustice is shown to any one. The only taxes that the Uitlanders are compelled to pay are the annual poll tax of less than four dollars and a half, mining taxes of a dollar and a quarter a month for each claim for prospecting licenses, and five dollars a claim for diggers' licenses. Boer and Uitlander are compelled to pay these taxes without distinction.

The Boers, in this contention, must win or die. In earlier days, before every inch of African soil was under the flag of one country or another, they were able to escape from English injustice by loading their few possessions on wagons and "trekking" into new and unexplored lands. If they yield their country to the English without a struggle, they will be forced to live under a future Stock Exchange Government, which has been described by a member of the British Parliament as likely to be "the vilest, the most corrupt, and the most pernicious known to man." *

The Boers have no better argument to advance in support of their claim than that which is contained in the Transvaal national hymn. It at once gives a history of their country, its many struggles and disappointments, and its hopes. It is written in the "taal" of the coun-

---

* The Hon. Henry Labouchere, in London Truth.

try, and when sung by the patriotic, deep-voiced Boers is one of the most impressive hymns that ever inspired a nation.

THE TRANSVAAL VOLKSLIED.

The four-colours of our dear old land
    Again float o'er Transvaal,
And woe the God-forgetting hand
    That down our flag would haul!
Wave higher now in clearer sky
    Our Transvaal freedom's stay!
        (Lit., freedom's flag.)
Our enemies with fright did fly;
    Now dawns a glorious day.

Through many a storm ye bravely stood,
    And we stood likewise true;
Now, that the storm is o'er, we would
    Leave nevermore from you
Bestormed by Kaffir, Lion, Brit,
    Wave ever o'er their head;
And then to spite we hoist thee yet
    Up to the topmost stead!

Four long years did we beg—aye, pray—
    To keep our lands clear, free,
We asked you, Brit, we loath the fray:
    "Go hence, and let us be!
We've waited, Brit, we love you not,
    To arms we call the Boer;"
        (Lit., Now take we to our guns.)
"You've teased us long enough, we troth,
    Now wait we nevermore.".

And with God's help we cast the yoke
  Of England from our knee;
Our country safe—behold and look—
  Once more our flag waves free!
Though many a hero's blood it cost,
  May all the nations see
    (Lit., Though England ever so much more.)
That God the Lord redeemed our hosts;
  The glory his shall be.

Wave high now o'er our dear old land,
  Wave four-colours of Transvaal!
And woe the God-forgetting hand
  That dares you down to haul!
Wave higher now in clearer sky
  Our Transvaal freedom's stay!
Our enemies with fright did fly;
  Now dawns a glorious day.

CHAPTER X

PREPARATIONS FOR DEFENCE

EVER since the Jameson raid both the Boers and the Uitlanders have realized that a peaceful solution of the differences between the two is possible but highly improbable. The Uitlanders refused to concede anything to the Boer, and asked for concessions that implied a virtual abandonment of their country to the English, whom they have always detested. The Boers themselves have not been unmindful of the inevitable war with their powerful antagonist, and, not unlike the tiny ant of the African desert, which fortifies its abode against the anticipated attack of wild beasts, have made of their country a veritable arsenal.

Probably no inland country in the world is half so well prepared for war at any time as that little Government, which can boast of having less than thirty thousand voters. The military preparation has been so enormous that Great Britain has been compelled, according to the colonial secretary's statement to the British Parliament, to expend two and a half million dollars annually in South Africa in order to keep pace with the Boers. Four years ago, when the Transvaal Government learned that the Uitlanders of Johannesburg were planning a revolution, it commenced the military preparations which have ever since continued with unabating vigour. German experts were employed to formulate plans for the defence of the country, and European artillerists were secured to teach the arts of modern warfare to the men at the head of the Boer army. Several Americans of military training became the instructors in the national military school at Pretoria; and even the women and children became imbued with the necessity of warlike preparation, and learned the use of arms. Several million pounds were annually spent in Europe in the purchase of the armament required by the plans formulated by the experts, and the whole country was placed on a war footing. Every important strategic position was made as impregnable as modern skill and arms could make it, and every farmer's cottage was supplied with arms and ammunition, so that the volunteer army might be mobilized in a day.

In order to demonstrate the extent to which the military preparation has been carried, it is only necessary to give an account of the defences of Pretoria and Johannesburg, the two principal cities of the country. Pretoria, being the capital, and naturally the chief point of attack by the enemy, has been prepared to resist the onslaught of any number of men, and is in a condition to withstand a siege of three years. The city lies in the centre of a square, at each corner of which is a lofty hill surmounted by a strong fort, which commands the valleys and the surrounding country. Each of the four forts has four heavy cannon, four French guns of fifteen miles range, and thirty heavy Gatling guns. Besides this extraordinary protection, the city has fifty light Gatling guns which can be drawn by mules to any point on the hills where an attack may be made. Three large warehouses are filled with ammunition, and the large armory is packed to the eaves with Mauser, Martini-Henry, and Wesley-Richards rifles. Two extensive refrigerators, with a capacity of two thousand oxen each, are ample provision against a siege of many months. It is difficult to compute the total expenditures for war material by the Boer Government during the last four years, but the following official announcement of expenses for one year will serve to give an idea of the vastness of the preparations that the Government has been compelled to make in order to guard the safety of the country:

War-Office salaries	$262,310
War purposes	4,717,550
Johannesburg revolt	800,000
Public works	3,650,000
	$9,429,860

Johannesburg has extensive fortifications around it, but the Boers will use them for other purposes than those of self-protection. The forts at the Golden City were erected for the purpose of quelling any revolution of the

Uitlanders, who constitute almost entirely the population of the city.

One of the forts is situated on a small eminence about half a mile north of the business part, and commands the entire city with its guns. Two years were consumed in building the fortification and in placing the armament in position. Its guns can rake not only every street of the city, but ten of the principal mine works as well, and the damage that their fire could cause is incalculable. Another fort, almost as strong as the one in Johannesburg, is situated a mile east of the city, and overshadows the railway and the principal highway to Johannesburg. The residents of the city are greatly in fear of underground works, which they have been led to believe were constructed since the raid. Vast quantities of earth were taken out of the Johannesburg fort, and for such a length of time did the work continue that the Uitlanders decided that the Boers were undermining the city, and protested to the Government against such a course. As soon as war is declared and the women and children have been removed from the city, Johannesburg will be rent with shot and shell. The Boers have announced their intention of doing this, and the Uitlanders, anticipating it, seek safety in flight whenever there are rumours of war, as thousands did immediately before and after the Jameson affair.

The approaches to the mountain passes on the border have been fortified with vast quantities of German and French ordnance, and equipped with garrisons of men born or trained in Europe. The approaches to Laing's Nek, near the Natal border, which have several times been the battle ground of the English and Boer forces, have been prepared to resist an invading army from Natal. Much attention has been directed to the preparations in that part of the republic, because the British commanders will find it easier to transfer forces from the port of Durban, which is three hundred and six miles from the Transvaal border, while Cape Town is almost a thousand miles distant.

But the Pretorian Government has made many provisions for war other than those enumerated. It has made alliances and friends that will be of equal worth in the event of an attack by England. The Orange Free State, whose existence is as gravely imperilled as that of the Transvaal, will fight hand-in-hand with its neighbour, just as it was prepared to do at the time of the Jameson raid, when almost every Free State burgher lay armed on the south bank of the Vaal River, awaiting the summons for assistance from the Kruger Government. In the event of war the two Governments will be as one, and, in anticipation of the struggle of the Boers against the British, the Free State Government has been expending vast sums of money every year in strengthening the country's defences. At the same time that the Free State is being prepared for war, its Government officials are striving hard to prevent a conflict, and are attempting to conciliate the two principals in the strife by suggesting that concessions be made by both. The Free State is not so populous as the Transvaal, and consequently can not place as many men in the field, but the ten thousand burghers who will

PREPARATIONS FOR DEFENCE 243

answer the call to arms will be an acceptable addition to the Boer forces.

The element of doubt enters into the question of what the Boers and their co-religionists of Cape Colony and Natal will do in the event of war. The Dutch of Cape Colony are the majority of the population, and, although loyal British subjects under ordinary circumstances, are opposed to English interference in the Transvaal's affairs. Those of Natal, while not so great in numbers, are equally friendly with the Transvaal Boers, and would undoubtedly recall some of their old grievances against the British Government as sufficient reason to join the Boers in war.

In Cape Colony there is an organization called the Afrikander Bond which recently has gained control of the politics of the colony, and which will undoubtedly be supreme for many years to come. The motto of the organization is "South Africa for South Africans," and its doctrine is that South Africa shall be served first and Great Britain afterward. Its members, who are chiefly Dutch, believe their first duty is to assist the development of the resources of their own country by proper protective tariffs and stringent legislation in native affairs, and they regard legislation with a view to British interests as of secondary importance. The Bond has been very amicably inclined toward its Afrikander kinsmen in the Transvaal, especially since the Jameson raid, and every sign of impending trouble between England and the Boers widens the chasm between the English and Afrikanders of South Africa. The Dutch approve of President Kruger's course in dealing with the franchise problems, and if hostilities break out it would be not the least incompatible with their natures to assist their Transvaal and Free State kinsmen even at the risk of plunging the whole of South Africa into a civil war. W. P. Schreiner, the Premier of Cape Colony, is the leading member of the Bond, and with him he has associated the majority of the leading men in the colony. Under ordinary conditions their loyalty to Great Britain is undoubted, but whether they could resist the influence of their friends in the Bond if it should decide to cast its fortunes with the Boers in case of war is another matter.

Of such vast importance is the continued loyalty of the Dutch of the two colonies that upon it depends practically the future control of the Cape by the British Government. Being in the majority as three to two, and almost in supreme control of the local government, the Dutch of Cape Colony are in an excellent position to secede from the empire, as they have already threatened to do, in which event England would be obliged to fight almost the united population of the whites if she desired to retain control of the country. With this in mind, it is no wonder that Mr. Chamberlain declared that England had reached a critical turning point in the history of the empire.

The uncertainty of the situation is increased by the doubtful stand which the native races are taking in the dispute. Neither England nor the Boers has the positive assurance of support from any of the tribes, which outnumber the whites as ten to one; but it will not be an unwarranted opinion to place the majority of the native tribes on the side of the Boers. The native races are always eager to be the friends of the paramount power, and England's many defeats in South Africa during recent years have not assisted in gaining for it that prestige. When England enters upon a war with the Transvaal the natives will probably follow the example of the Matabele natives, who rebelled against the English immediately after Jameson and his men were defeated by the Boers, because they believed a conquered nation could offer no resistance. The Boers, having won the last battle, are considered by the natives to be the paramount power, and it is always an easy matter to induce a subjected people to ally itself with a supposedly powerful one.

The Zulus, still stinging under the defeat which they received from the British less than twenty years ago, might gather their war parties and, with the thousands of guns they have been allowed to buy, attempt to secure revenge. The Basutos, east of the Orange Free State, now the most powerful and the only undefeated nation in the country, would hardly allow a war to be fought unless they participated in it, even if only to demonstrate to the white man that they still retain their old-time courage and ability. The million and a half natives in Cape Colony, and the equal number in the Transvaal, have complained of so many alleged grievances at the hands of their respective governments that they might be presumed to rise against them, though it is never possible to determine the trend of the African negro's mind. What the various tribes would do in such an emergency can be answered only by the chiefs themselves, and they will not speak until the time for action is at hand. Perhaps when that time does arrive there may be a realization of the natives' dream—that a great leader will. come from the north who will organize all the various tribes into one grand army and with it drive the hated white men into the sea.

It is impossible to secure accurate statistics in regard to the military strength of the various colonies, states, and tribes in the country, but the following table gives a fair idea of the number of men who are liable to military duty:

	Dutch.	English.	Native.
Cape Colony...................	20,000	10,000	175,000
Natal.........................	7,000	5,000	100,000
Orange Free State.............	10,000	....	30,000
Transvaal.....................	30,000	20,000	140,000
Rhodesia	....	2,000	25,000
Swaziland and Basutoland......	....	....	30,000
Total......................	67,000	37,000	570,000

To him who delights in forming possible coalitions and war situations this table offers vast opportunities. Probably no other country can offer such a vast number of possibilities for compacts between nations, races, and tribes as is presented in South Africa. There all the natives may unite against the whites, or a part of them against a part of the whites, while whites and natives may unite against a similar combination. The possibilities are boundless; the probabilities are uncertain.

The Pretorian Government has had an extensive secret service for several years, and this has been of inestimable value in securing the support of the natives as well as the friendship of many whites, both in South Af-

'rica and abroad. The several thousand Irishmen in South Africa have been organized into a secret compact, and have been and will continue to be of great value to the Boers. The head of the organization is a man who is one of President Kruger's best friends, and his lieutenants are working even as far away as America. The sympathy of the majority of the Americans in the Transvaal is with the Boer cause, and, although the American consul-general at Cape Town has cautioned them to remain neutral, they will not stand idly by and watch the defeat of a cause which they believe to be as just as that for which their forefathers fought at Bunker Hill and Lexington.

But the Boers do not rely upon external assistance to win their battles for them. When it becomes necessary to defend their liberty and their country they reverently place their trust in Providence and their rifles. Their forefathers' battles were won with such confidence, and the later generations have been similarly successful under like conditions. The rifle is the young Boer's primer and the grandfather's testament. It is the Boers' avenger of wrong and the upholder of right. That their confidence in their rifles has not been misapplied has been demonstrated at Laing's Nek, Majuba Hill, Doornkop, and in battles with natives.

The natural opportunities provided by Nature which in former years were responsible for the confidence which the Boers reposed in their rifles may have disappeared with the approach of advancing civilization, but the Boer of to-day is as dangerous an adversary with a gun as his father was in the wars with the Zulus and the Matabeles half a century ago. The buck, rhinoceros, elephant, and hippopotamus are not as numerous now as then, but the Boer has devised other means by which he may perfect himself in marksmanship. Shooting is one of the main diversions of the Boer, and prizes are offered for the best results in contests. It is customary to mark out a ring, about two hundred and fifty feet in diameter, in the centre of which a small stuffed figure resembling a bird is attached to a pole. The marksmen stand on the outside of the circle and fire in turn at the target. A more curious target, and one that taxes the ability of the marksman, is in more general use throughout the country. A hole sufficiently deep to retain a turkey-cock is dug in a level plot of ground, and over this is placed a piece of canvas which contains a small hole through which the bird can extend and withdraw its head. At a distance of three hundred feet the bird's head is a target by no means easily hit.

Military men are accustomed to sneer at the lack of generalship of the Boer forces, but in only one of the battles in which they have engaged the British forces have the trained military men and leaders been able to cope with them. In the battle of Boomplaats, fought in 1848, the English officers can claim their only victory over the Boers, who were armed with flintlocks, while the British forces had heavy artillery. In almost all the encounters that have taken place the Boer forces were not as large as those of the enemy, yet the records show that many more casualties were inflicted than received by them. In the chief engagements the appended statistics show that the Boers had only a small percentage of their men in the casualty list, while the British losses were much greater.

BATTLES.	MEN ENGAGED.		CASUALTIES.	
	British.	Boer.	British.	Boer.
Laing's Nek	400	550	190	24
Ingogo	300	250	142	17
Majuba Hill	600	150	280	5
Bronkhorst	250	300	120	1
Jameson raid	600	400	100	5

It is hardly fair to assume that the Boers' advantages in these battles were gained without the assistance of capable generals when it is taken into consideration that there is a military axiom which places the value of an army relatively with the ability of its commanders. The Boers may exaggerate when they assert that one of their soldiers is the equal in fighting ability of five British soldiers, but the results of the various battles show that they have some slight foundation for their theory.

The regular British force in South Africa is comparatively small, but it would require less than a month to transport one hundred thousand trained soldiers from India and England and place them on the scene of action. Several regiments of trained soldiers are always stationed in different parts of the country near the Transvaal border, and at brief notice they could be placed on Boer territory. Charlestown, Ladysmith, and Pietermaritzburg, in Natal, have been British military headquarters for many years, and during the last three years they have been strengthened by the addition of several regular regiments. The British Colonial Office has been making preparations for several years for a conflict. Every point in the country has been strengthened, and all the foreign powers whose interests in the country might lead them to interfere in behalf of the Boers have been placated. Germany has been taken from the British zone of danger by favourable treaties; France is fearful to try interference alone; and Portugal, the only other nation interested, is too weak and too deeply in England's debt to raise her voice against anything that may be done.

By leasing the town of Lorenzo Marques from the Portuguese Government, Great Britain has acquired one of the best strategic points in South Africa. The lease, the terms of which are unannounced, was the culmination of much diplomatic dickering, in which the interests of Germany and the South African Republic were arrayed against those of England and Portugal. There is no doubt that England made the lease only in order to gain an advantage over President Kruger, and to prevent him from further fortifying his country with munitions of war imported by way of Lorenzo Marques and Delagoa Bay. England gains a commercial advantage too, but it is hardly likely that she would care to add the worst fever-hole in Africa to her territory simply to please the few of her merchants who have business interests in the town.

Since the Jameson raid the Boers have been purchasing vast quantities of guns and ammunition in Europe for the purpose of preparing themselves for any similar emergency. Delagoa Bay alone was an open port to the Transvaal, every other port in South Africa being under English dominion and consequently closed to the importation of war material. Lorenzo Marques, the natural port of the Transvaal, is only a short distance from the eastern border of that country, and is connected with Pretoria and Johannesburg by a railway. It was over this railway that the Boers were able to carry the guns and ammunition with which to fortify their country, and England could not raise a finger to prevent the little republic from doing as it pleased. Hardly a month has passed since the raid that the Transvaal authorities did not receive a large consignment of guns and powder from Germany and France by way of Lorenzo Marques. England could do nothing more than have several detectives at the docks to take an inventory of the munitions as they passed in transit.

The transfer of Lorenzo Marques to the British will put an effectual bar to any further importation of guns into the Transvaal, and will practically prevent any foreign assistance from reaching the Boers in the event of another war. Both Germany and England tried for many years to induce Portugal to sell Delagoa Bay, but being the debtor of both to a great extent, the sale could not be made to one without arousing the enmity of the other. Eighteen or twenty years ago Portugal would have sold her sovereign right over the port to Mr. Gladstone's Government for sixty thousand dollars, but that was before Delagoa Bay had any commercial or political importance. Since then Germany became the political champion of the Transvaal, and blocked all the schemes of England to isolate the inland country by cutting off its only neutral connection with the sea. Recently, however, Germany has been disappointed by the Transvaal Republic, and one of the results is the present cordial relations between the Teutons and the Anglo-Saxons in South African affairs.

The English press and people in South Africa have always asserted that by isolating the Transvaal from the sea the Boers could be starved into submission in case of a war. As soon as the lease becomes effective, Mr. Kruger's country will be completely surrounded by English territory, at least in such a way that nothing can be taken into the Transvaal without first passing through an English port, and no foreign power will be able to send forces to the aid of the Boers unless they are first landed on British soil. It is doubtful whether any nation would incur such a grave responsibility for the sake of securing Boer favour.

Both the Transvaal and England are fully prepared for war, and diplomacy only can postpone its coming. The Uitlanders' present demands may be conceded, but others that will follow may not fare so well. A coveted country will always be the object of attacks by a stronger power, and the aggressor generally succeeds in securing from the weaker victim whatever he desires. Whether British soldiers will be obliged to fight the Boers alone in order to gratify the wishes of their Government, or whether the enemy will be almost the entire white and black population of South Africa, will not be definitely known until the British troop ships start for Cape Town and Durban.

Whichever enemy it will be, the British Government will attack, and will pursue in no half-hearted or half-prepared manner, as it has done in previous campaigns in the country. The Boers will be able to resist and to prolong the campaign to perhaps eight months or a year, but they will finally be obliterated from among the nations of the earth. It will cost the British Empire much treasure and many lives, but it will satisfy those who caused it—the politicians and speculators.

Cape Town and Table Mountain.

CHAPTER XI

AMERICAN INTERESTS IN SOUTH AFRICA

An idea of the nature and extent of American enterprise in South Africa might be deduced from the one example of a Boston book agent, who made a competency by selling albums of United States scenery to the negroes along the shores of the Umkomaas River, near Zululand. The book agent is not an incongruity of the activity of Americans in that part of the continent, but an example rather of the diversified nature of the influences which owe their origin to the nation of Yankees ten thousand miles distant. The United States of America have had a deeper influence upon South Africa than that which pertains to commerce and trade. The progress, growth, and prosperity of the American States have instilled in the minds of the majority of South Africans a desire to be free from European control, and to be united under a single banner, which is to bear the insignia of the United States of South Africa.

In public, editors and speechmakers in Cape Colony, Natal, and the Transvaal spend hours in deploring the progress of Americanisms in South Africa, but in their clubs and libraries they study and discuss the causes which led to America's progress and pre-eminence, and form plans by which they may be able to attain the same desirable ends. The influence and example of the United States are not theoretical; they are political factors which are felt in the discussion of every public question and in the results of every election. The practical results of American influence in South Africa may now be observed only in the increasing exports to that country, but perhaps in another generation a greater and better demonstration will be found in a constitution which unites all the South African states under one independent government. If any corroboration of this sentiment were necessary, a statement made by the man who is leader of the ruling party in Cape Colony would be ample.

AMERICAN INTERESTS IN SOUTH AFRICA 261

"If we want an example of the highest type of freedom," said W. P. Schreiner, the present Premier of Cape Colony, "we must look to the United States of America."*

American influences are felt in all phases of South African life, be they social, commercial, religious, political, or retrogressive. Whether it be the American book agent on the banks of the Umkomaas, or the American consul-general in the governor's mansion at Cape Town, his indomitable energy, his breezy indifference to apparently insurmountable difficulties, and his boundless resources will always secure for him those material benefits for which men of other nationalities can do no more than hope. Some of his rivals call it perverseness, callousness, trickery, treachery, and what not; his admirers might ascribe his success to energy, pluck, modern methods, or to that quality best described by that Americanism—"hustling."

American commercial interests in South Africa are of such recent growth, and already of such great proportions, that the other na-

---

* Americans' Fourth of July Banquet, Cape Town, 1897.

tions who have been interested in the trade for many years are not only astounded, but are fearful that the United States will soon be the controlling spirit in the country's commercial affairs. The enterprise of American business firms, and their ability to undersell almost all the other firms represented in the country, have given an enormous impetus to the export trade with South African countries. Systematic efforts have been made by American firms to work the South African markets on an extensive scale, and so successful have the efforts been that the value of exports to that country has several times been more than doubled in a single year.

Five years ago America's share of the business of South Africa was practically infinitesimal; to-day the United States hold second place in the list of nations which have trade relations with that country, having outranked Germany, France, Belgium, Holland, and Italy. In several branches of trade America surpasses even England, which has always had all the trade advantages owing to the supremacy of her flag over the greater part of the country.

That the British merchants are keenly alive to the situation which threatens to transfer the trade supremacy into American hands has been amply demonstrated by the efforts which they have made to check the inroads the Americans are making on their field, and by the appointment of committees to investigate the causes of the decline of British commerce.

American enterprise shows itself by the scores of representatives of American business houses who are constantly travelling through the country, either to secure orders or to investigate the field with a view of entering into competition with the firms of other nations. Fifteen American commercial travellers, representing as many different firms, were registered at the Grand Hotel, Cape Town, at one time a year ago, and that all had secured exceptionally heavy orders indicated that the innovation in the method of working trade was successful.

The laws of the country are unfavourable in no slight degree to the foreign commercial travellers, who are obliged to pay heavy licenses before they are permitted to enter upon any business negotiations. The tax in the Transvaal and Natal is $48.66, and in the Orange Free State and Cape Colony it amounts to $121.66. If an American agent wishes to make a tour of all the states and colonies of the country, he is obliged to pay almost three hundred and fifty dollars in license fees.

The great superiority of certain American manufactured products is such that other nations are unable to compete in those lines after the American products have been introduced. Especially is this true of American machinery, which can not be equalled by that of any other country. Almost every one of the hundreds of extensive gold mines on the Randt is fitted out wholly or in part with American machinery, and, at the present rate of increase in the use of it, it will be less than ten years when none other than United States machinery will be sent to that district. In visiting the great mines the uninitiated American is astonished to find that engines, crushing machinery, and even the electric lights which illuminate them, bear the name plates of New York, Philadelphia, and Chicago firms.

The Kimberley diamond mines, which are among the most extensive and most elaborate underground works in the world, use American-made machinery almost exclusively, not only because it is much less costly, but because no other country can furnish apparatus that will give as good results. Almost every pound of electrical machinery in use in the country was made in America and was instituted by American workmen.

Instances of successful American electrical enterprises are afforded by the Cape Town, Port Elizabeth, and Pretoria street railways, almost every rail, wire, and car of which bears the marks of American manufacture. It is a marvellous revelation to find Philadelphia-made electric cars in the streets of Cape Town, condensing engines from New York State in Port Elizabeth, and Pittsburg generators and switchboards in the capital of the Transvaal, which less than fifty years ago was under the dominion of savages. Not only did Americans install the street railways, but they also secured the desirable concessions for operating the lines for a stated period. American electricians operate the plants, and in not a few instances have financially embarrassed Americans received a new financial impetus by acting in the capacities of motormen and conductors.

One street car in Cape Town was for a long time distinguished because of its many American features. The Philadelphia-made car was propelled over Pittsburg tracks by means of the power passing through Wilkesbarre wires, and the human agencies that controlled it were a Boston motorman and a San Francisco conductor. It might not be pursuing the subject too far to add that of the twelve passengers in the car on a certain journey ten were Americans, representing eight different States.

One of the first railroads in South Africa—that which leads from Lorenzo Marques to the Transvaal border—was built by an American, a Mr. Murdock, while American material entered largely into the construction of the more extensive roads from the coast to the interior. American rails are more quickly and more cheaply * obtainable in South Africa than those

---

* " But the other day we gave an order for two hundred and fifty miles of rails. We had a large number of tenders,

of English make, but the influence which is exerted against the use of other than British rails prevents their universal adoption. Notwithstanding the efforts of the influential Englishmen to secure British manufactures wherever and whenever possible, American firms have recently secured the contracts for forty thousand tons of steel rails for the Cape Colony Railway system, and the prospects are that more orders of a similar nature will be forthcoming.

It is not in the sale of steel rails alone that the American manufacturer is forging ahead of his competitors in South Africa. American manufactured wares of all kinds are in demand, and in many instances they are leaders in the market. Especially true is this of American agricultural implements, which are so much more adaptable to the soil and much cheaper than any other make. Small stores in the

---

and the lowest tender, you may be sorry to hear, was sent by an American, Mr. Carnegie. Fortunately, however, the tender was not in order, and we were therefore able to give the work to our own people. It may be said that this American tender was a question of workmen and strikes."
—Cecil J. Rhodes, at a meeting of the stockholders of the Cape-Cairo Railway, London, May 2, 1899.

farming communities of Natal and Cape Colony sell American ploughshares, spades, forks, rakes, and hoes almost exclusively, and it amazes the traveller to find that almost every plough and reaper used by the more progressive agriculturists bears the imprint "Made in the United States."

It is a strange fact that, although South Africa has vast areas covered with heavy timber, almost all the lumber used in the mining districts is transported thither from Puget Sound. The native timber being unsuited for underground purposes and difficult of access, all the mine owners are obliged to import every foot of wood used in constructing surface and underground works of their mines, and at great expense, for to the original cost of the timber is added the charges arising from the sea and land transportation, import duties, and handling. The docks at Cape Town almost all the year round contain one or more lumber vessels from Puget Sound, and upon several occasions five such vessels were being unloaded at the same time.

American coal, too, has secured a foothold in South Africa, a sample cargo of three thousand tons having been despatched thither at the beginning of the year. Coal of good quality is found in several parts of the Transvaal and Natal, but progress in the development of the mines has been so slow that almost the total demand is supplied by Wales. Cape Colony has an extensive petroleum field, but it is in the hands of *concessionnaires*, who, for reasons of their own, refuse to develop it. American and Russian petroleums are used exclusively, but the former is preferred, and is rapidly crowding the other out of the market.

Among the many other articles of export to South Africa are flour, corn, butter, potatoes, canned meats, and vegetables—all of which might be produced in the country if South Africans took advantage of the opportunities offered by soil and Nature. American live stock has been introduced into the country since the rinderpest disease destroyed almost all of the native cattle, and with such successful results that several Western firms have established branches in Cape Town, and are sending thither large cargoes of mules, horses, cattle, and sheep. Cecil J. Rhodes has recently stocked his immense Rhodesian farm with American live stock, and, as his example is generally followed throughout the country, a decided increase in the live-stock export trade is anticipated.

Statistics only can give an adequate idea of American trade with South Africa; but even these are not reliable, for the reason that a large percentage of the exports sent to the country are ordered through London firms, and consequently do not appear in the official figures. As a criterion of what the trade amounts to, it will only be necessary to quote a few statistics, which, however, do not represent the true totals for the reason given. The estimated value of the exports and the percentage increase of each year's business over that of the preceding year is given, in order that a true idea of the growth of American trade with South Africa may be formed:

Year.	Value.	Per cent increase.
1895	$5,000,000	
1896	12,000,000	140
1897	16,000,000	33½
1898 (estimated)	20,000,000	25

A fact that is deplored by Americans who are eager to see their country in the van in all things pertaining to trade is that almost every dollar's worth of this vast amount of material is carried to South Africa in ships sailing under foreign colours. Three lines of steamships, having weekly sailings, ply between the two countries, and are always laden to the rails with American goods, but the American flag is carried by none of them. A fourth line of steamships, to ply between Philadelphia and Cape Town, is about to be established under American auspices, and is to carry the American flag. A number of small American sailing vessels trade between the two countries, but their total capacity is so small as to be almost insignificant when compared with the great volume carried in foreign bottoms.

The American imports from South Africa are of far less value than the exports, for the reason that the country produces only a few articles that are not consumed where they originate. America is the best market in the world for diamonds, and about one fourth of the annual output of the Kimberley mines reaches the United States. Hides and tallow constitute the leading exportations to America, while aloes and ostrich feathers are chief among the few other products sent here. Owing to this lack of exports, ships going to South Africa are obliged to proceed to India or Australia for return cargoes in order to reduce the expenses of the voyage.

However great the commercial interests of the United States in South Africa, they are small in comparison with the work of individual Americans, who have been active in the development of that country during the last quarter of a century. Wherever great enterprises have been inaugurated, Americans have been prominently identified with their growth and development, and in not a few instances has the success of the ventures been wholly due to American leadership. European capital is the foundation of all the great South African institutions, but it is to American skill that almost all of them owe the success which they have attained.

British and continental capitalists have recognised the superiority of American methods by intrusting the management of almost every large mine and industry to men who were born and received their training in the United States. It is an expression not infrequently heard when the success of a South African enterprise is being discussed, "Who is the Yankee?" The reason of this is involved in the fact that almost all the Americans who went to South Africa after the discovery of gold had been well fitted by their experiences in the California and Colorado mining fields for the work which they were called upon to do on the Randt, and, owing to their ability, were able to compete successfully with the men from other countries who were not so skilled.

Unfortunately, not all the Americans in South Africa have been a credit to their native country, and there is a considerable class which has created for itself an unenviable reputation. The component parts of this class are men who, by reason of criminal acts, were obliged to leave America for new fields of endeavour, and non-professional men who follow gold booms in all parts of the world and trust to circumstances for a livelihood. In the early days of the Johannesburg gold fields these men oftentimes resorted to desperate means, with the result that almost every criminal act of an unusually daring description is now credited against them by the orderly inhabitants. Highwaymen, pickpockets, illicit gold buyers, confidence men, and even train-robbers were active, and for several years served to discredit the entire American colony. Since the first gold excitement has subsided, this class of Americans, in which was also included by the residents all the other criminal characters of whatever nationality, has been compelled to leave the country, and to-day the American colony in Johannesburg numbers about three thousand of the most respected citizens of the city.

The American who has been most prominent in South African affairs, and the stanchest supporter of American interests in that country, is Gardner F. Williams, the general manager and one of the alternate life governors of the De Beers Consolidated Diamond Mines at Kimberley. A native of Michigan, Mr. Williams gained his mining experience in the mining districts of California and other Western States, and went to South Africa in 1887 to take charge of the Kimberley mines, which were then in an almost chaotic condition. By the application of American ideas, Mr. Williams succeeded in making of the mines a property which yields an annual profit of about ten million dollars on a nominal capital of twice that amount. He has introduced American machinery into the mines, and has been instrumental in many other ways in advancing the interests of his native country. Although Mr. Williams receives a salary twice as great as that of the President of the United States, he is proud to be the American consular agent at Kimberley—an office which does not carry with it sufficient revenue to provide the star-spangled banner which constantly floats from a staff in front of his residence.

Dr. J. Perrott Prince is another American who has assisted materially in extending American interests in South Africa, and it is due to his own unselfish efforts that the commerce of the United States with the port of Durban has risen from insignificant volume to its present size. Dr. Prince was a surgeon in the Union army during the civil war, and afterward was one of the first Americans to go to the Kimberley diamond fields. He it was who later induced Dr. Leander Starr Jameson to accompany him to Kimberley in the capacity of assistant surgeon—a service which he performed with great distinction until Mr. Rhodes sent him into Matabeleland to take charge of the military forces, which later he led into the Transvaal.

Dr. Prince's renown as a physician was responsible for a call to Madagascar, whither he was summoned by Queen Ranavalo. He remained in Madagascar as the queen's physician until the French took forcible possession of the island and sent the queen into exile on the Réunion Islands. Dr. Prince has lived in Durban, Natal, for several years, and during the greater part of that time conducted the office of American consular agent at a financial loss to himself. Unfortunately, Dr. Prince was obliged to end his connection with the consular service, and the United States are now represented in Durban by a foreigner, who on the last Fourth of July inquired why all the Americans in the city were making such elaborate displays of bunting and the Stars and Stripes.

The consular agent at Johannesburg is John C. Manion, of Herkimer, N. Y., who represents a large American machinery company. Mr. Manion, in 1896, carried on the negotiations with the Transvaal Government by which John Hays Hammond, an American mining engineer, was released from the Pretoria prison, where he had been confined for complicity in the uprising at Johannesburg. American machinery valued at several million dollars has been sent to South Africa as the result of Mr. Manion's efforts.

In the gold industry on the Randt, Americans have been specially active, and it is due to one of them, J. S. Curtis, that the deep-level mines were discovered. In South Africa a mining claim extends only a specified distance below the surface of the earth, and the Governments do not allow claim-owners to dig beyond that depth. Mr. Curtis found that paying reefs existed below the specified depth, and the result was that the Government sold the underground or deep-level claims with great profit to itself and the mining community.

The consulting engineers of almost all the mines of any importance in the country are Americans, and their salaries range from ten thousand to one hundred thousand dollars a year. John Hays Hammond, who was one of the first American engineers to reach the gold fields, was official mining engineer for the Transvaal Government, and received a yearly salary of twenty-five thousand dollars for formulating the mining laws of the country. He resigned that office, and is now the consulting engineer for the British South Africa Company in Rhodesia and several gold mines on the Randt, at salaries which aggregate almost one hundred thousand dollars a year. Among the scores of other American engineers on the Randt are L. I. Seymour, who has control of the thirty-six shafts of the Randt Mines; Captain Malan, of the Robinson mines; and H. S. Watson, of the Simmer en Jack mines, in developing which more than ten million dollars have been spent.

Another American introduced the system of

treating the abandoned tailings of the mines by the cyanide process, whereby thousands of ounces of gold have been abstracted from the offal of the mills, which had formerly been considered valueless. Others have revolutionized different parts of the management of the mines, and in many instances have taken abandoned properties and placed them on a paying basis. It would not be fair to claim that American ingenuity and skill are responsible for the entire success of the Randt gold mines, but it is indisputable that Americans have done more toward it than the combined representatives of all other nations.

Every line of business on the Randt has its American representatives, and almost without exception the firms who sent them thither chose able men. W. E. Parks, of Chicago, represents Frazer & Chalmers, whose machinery is in scores of the mines. His assistant is W. H. Haig, of New York city.

The American Trading and Importing Company, with its headquarters in Johannesburg, and branches in every city and town in the country, deals exclusively in American manufactured products, and annually sells immense quantities of bicycles, stoves, beer, carriages, and other goods, ranging from pins to pianos.

Americans do not confine their endeavours to commercial enterprises, and they may be found conducting missionary work among the Matabeles and Mashonas, as well as building dams in Rhodesia. American missionaries are very active in all parts of South Africa, and because of the practical methods by which they endeavour to civilize and Christianize the natives they have the reputation throughout the country of being more successful than those who go there from any other country. In the Rhodesian country Mr. Rhodes has given many contributions of land and money to the American missionaries, and has on several occasions complimented them by pronouncing, their achievements unparalleled.

A practical illustration will demonstrate the causes of the success of the American missionary. An English missionary spent the first two years after his arrival in the country in studying the natives' language and in building a house for himself. In that time he had made no converts. An American missionary arrived at almost the same time, rented a hut, and hired interpreters. At the end of two years he had one hundred and fifty converts, many more natives who were learning useful occupations and trades, and had sent home a request for more missionaries with which to extend his field.

It is rather remarkable that the scouts who assisted in subduing the American Indians should later be found on the African continent to assist in the extermination of the blacks. In the Matabele and Mashona campaigns of three years ago, Americans who scouted for Custer and Miles on the Western plains were invaluable adjuncts to the British forces, and in many instances did heroic work in finding the location of the enemy and in making way for the American Maxim guns that were used in the campaigns.

The Americans in South Africa, although only about ten thousand in number, have been of invaluable service to the land. They have taught the farmers to farm, the miners to dig gold, and the statesmen to govern.

Their work has been a credit to the country which they continue to revere, and whose flag they raise upon every proper occasion. They have taken little part in the political disturbances of the Transvaal, because they believe that the citizens of a republic should be allowed to conduct its government according to their own idea of right and justice, independently of the demands of those who are not citizens.

CHAPTER XII

JOHANNESBURG OF TO-DAY

THE palms and bamboos of Durban, the Zulu policemen and 'ricksha boys, and the hospitable citizens have been left behind, and the little train of English compartment cars, each with its destination "Johannesburg" labelled conspicuously on its sides, is winding away through cane fields and banana groves, past groups of open-eyed natives and solemn, thin-faced Indian coolies.

Pretty little farmers' cottages in settings of palms, mimosas, and tropical plants are dotted in the green valleys winding around the innumerable small hills that look for all the world like so many inverted moss-covered china cups. Lumbering transport wagons behind a score of sleek oxen, wincing under the fire of the far-reaching rawhide in the hands of a sparsely clad Zulu driver, are met and passed in a twinkling. Neatly thatched huts with natives lazily lolling in the sun become more frequent as the train rolls on toward the interior, and the greenness of the landscape is changing into the brown of dead verdure, for it is the dry season—the South African winter. The hills become more frequent, and the little locomotive goes more slowly, while the train twists and writhes along its path like a huge python.

Now it is on the hilltop from which the distant sea and its coast fringe of green are visible on the one side, and nothing but treeless brown mountain tops on the other. A minute later it plunges down the hillside, along rocky precipices, over deep chasms, and then wearily plods up the zigzag course of another hillside. For five hours or more the monotony of miniature mountains continues, relieved by nothing more interesting than the noise of the train and the hilarious laughter and weird songs of a car load of Zulus bound for the gold fields. After this comes an undulating plain and towns with far less interest in their appearance than in their names. The

Zulu maidens shaking hands.

traveller surfeited with Natal scenery finds amusement and diversion in the conductor's call of Umbilo, Umkomaas, Umgeni, Amanzimtoti, Isipingo, Mooi River, Zwartkop, or Pietermaritzburg, but will not attempt to learn the proper pronunciation of the names unless he has weeks at his command.

Farther on in the journey an ostrich, escaped from a farm, stalks over the plain, and, approaching to within several yards of the train, jogs along for many miles, and perchance wheedles the engineer into impromptu races. Hardly has the bird disappeared when on the wide veldt a herd of buck galloping with their long heads down, or a large number of wildebeest, plunging and jumping like animated hobby-horses, raise clouds of dust as they dash away from the monster of iron and steam. Shortly afterward the train passes a waterfall almost thrice as lofty as Niagara, but located in the middle of the plain, into whose surface the water has riven a deep and narrow chasm.

Since the balmy Indian Ocean has been left behind, the train has been rising steadily, sometimes an inch in a mile but oftener a hundred feet, and the air has grown cooler. The thousands of British soldiers at Ladysmith are wearing heavy clothing; their horses, tethered in the open air, are shivering, and far to the westward is the cause of it all—the lofty, snow-covered peaks of the Dragon Mountain. Night comes on and clothes the craggy mountains and broken valleys with varying shades of sombreness. The moon outlines the snow far above, and with its rays marks the lofty line where sky and mountain crest seem to join. Morning light greets the train as it dashes down the mountain side, through the passes that connect Natal with the Transvaal and out upon the withered grass of the flat, uninteresting veldt of the Boer country.

The South African veldt in all its winter hideousness lies before you. It stretches out in all directions—to the north and south, to the east and west—and seems to have no boundaries. Its yellowish brownness eats into the brain, and the eyes grow weary from the monotony of the scene. Hour after hour the train bears onward in a straight line, but the

JOHANNESBURG OF TO-DAY

landscape remains the same. But for noises and motions of the cars you would imagine that the train was stationary, so far as change of scenery is concerned. Occasionally a colony of huge ant-heaps or a few buck or deer may be passed, but for hours it is veldt, veldt, veldt! An entire day's journey, unrelieved except toward the end by a few straggling towns of Boer farmhouses or the sheet-iron cabins of prospectors, bring it to Heidelberg, once the metropolis as well as the capital of the republic, but now pining because the former distinguishing mark has been yielded to its neighbour, Johannesburg.

As the shades of another night commence to fall, the veldt suddenly assumes a new countenance. Lights begin to sparkle, buildings close together appear, and scores of tall smoke-stacks tower against the background of the sky. The presence of the smoke-stacks denote the arrival at the Randt, and for twenty miles the train rushes along this well-defined gold-yielding strip of land. Buildings, lights, stacks, and people become more numerous as the train progresses into the city limits of Johannesburg, and the traveller soon finds himself in the middle of a crowd of enthusiastic welcoming and welcomed persons on the platform of the station of the Nederlandsche Zuid-Afrikaansche Spoorweg-Maatschappij, and in the Golden City.

The sudden change from the dreary lifelessness of the veldt to the exciting crush and bustle of the station platform crowd is almost bewildering, because it is so different from what is expected in interior Africa. The station, a magnificent structure of stone and iron, presents more animated scenes whenever trains arrive than the Grand Central in New York or the Victoria in London, because every passenger is invariably met at the train by all his friends and as many of their friends as the station platform will accommodate. The crowd which surges around this centre of the city's life is of a more cosmopolitan character than that which can be found in any other city in the world with the exceptions of Zanzibar and Port Said. Almost every race is represented in the gathering, which is suggestive of a mass meeting of the villagers of the Midway Plaisance at the Columbian Exposition. In the crowd are stolid Anglo-Saxons shaking hands effusively; enthusiastic Latins embracing each other; negroes rubbing noses and cheeks; smiling Japanese; cold, stern Chinese; Cingalese, Russians, Malays, and Egyptians—all in their national costumes, and all welcoming friends in their native manner and language. Meandering through the crowd are several keen-eyed Boer policemen, commonly called "Zarps," politely directing the attention of innocent-looking newcomers to placards bearing the inscription "Pas op Zakkenrollers," which is the Boer warning of pickpockets.

After the traveller has forced a way through the crowd he is attacked by a horde of cabmen who can teach tricks of the trade to the London and New York night-hawks. Their equipages range from dilapidated broughams to antique 'rickshas, but their charges are the same—"a quid," or five dollars, either for a mile or a minute's ride. After the insults which follow a refusal to enter one of their conveyances have subsided, the agents of the hotels commence a vociferous campaign against the newcomers, and very clever it is in its way. They are able to distinguish a foreigner at one glance, and will change the name of the hotel which they represent a score of times in as many seconds in order to bag their quarry. For the patriotic American they have the New York Hotel, the Denver House, the Hotel California, and many other hostelries named after American cities. " Hey, Yank! " they will salute an American, " Come up to the New York Hotel and patronize American enterprise." If the traveller will accompany one of these agents he will find that all the names apply to one hotel, which has an American name but is conducted and patronized by a low class of foreigners. The victim of misrepresentation will seek another hotel, and will be fortunate if he finds comfortable quarters for less than ten dollars a day, or three times the amount he would be called upon to pay at a far better hotel in any American city of equal size. The privilege of fasting, or of awakening in the morning with a layer of dust an eighth of an inch deep on the counterpane and on the face may be ample return for the extraordinary charges, but the stranger in the city is not apt to adopt that view of the situation until he is acclimated.

The person who has spent several days in crossing the veldt and enters Johannesburg by night has a strange revelation before him when he is awakened the following morning. He has been led to believe that the city is a motley collection of corrugated-iron hovels, hastily constructed cabins, and cheap public buildings. Instead he finds a beautiful city, with well-paved streets, magnificent buildings of stone and brick, expensive public buildings, and scores of palatial residences. Many American cities of the same size and many times older can not show as costly buildings or as fine public works. Hotels of five and six stories, and occupying, in several instances, almost entire blocks, are numerous; of office buildings costing a quarter of a million dollars each there are half a score; banks, shops, and newspapers have three- and four-story buildings of brick and stone, while there are hundreds of other buildings that would be creditable to any large city in America or Europe. The Government Building in the centre of the city is a five-story granite structure of no mean architectural beauty. In the suburbs are many magnificent private residences of mine owners and managers who, although not permanent residents of the city, have invested large amounts of money, so that the short time they spend in the country may be amid luxurious and comfortable surroundings.

One of the disagreeable features of living in Johannesburg is the dust which is present everywhere during the dry season. It rises in great, thick clouds on the surrounding veldt, and, obscuring the sun, wholly envelops the city in semi-darkness. One minute the air is clear and there is not a breath of wind; several minutes later a hurricane is blowing and blankets of dust are falling. The dust clouds generally rise west of the city, and almost totally eclipse the sun during their progress over the plain. Sometimes the dust storms continue only a few minutes, but very frequently the citizens are made uncomfortable by them for days at a time. Whenever they arrive, the doors and windows of buildings are tightly closed, business is practically at a standstill, and every one is miserable. There is no escape from it. It penetrates every building, however well protected, and it lodges in the food as well as in the drink. Pedestrians on the street are unable to see ten feet ahead, and are compelled to walk with head bowed and with handkerchief over the mouth and nostrils. Umbrellas and parasols are but slight protection against it. Only the miners, a thousand feet below the surface, escape it. When the storm has subsided the entire city is covered with a blanket of dust ranging in thickness from an inch on the sidewalks to an eighth of an inch on the store counters, furniture, and in pantries. It has never been computed how great a quantity of the dust enters a man's lungs, but the feeling that it engenders is one of colossal magnitude.

Second to the dust, the main characteristic of Johannesburg is the inhabitants' great struggle for sudden wealth. It is doubtful whether there is one person in the city whose ambition is less than to become wealthy in five years at least, and then to return to his native country. It is not a chase after affluence; it is a stampede in which every soul in the city endeavours to be in the van. In the city and in the mines there are hundreds of honourable ways of becoming rich, but there are thousands of dishonourable ones; and the morals of a mining city are not always on the highest plane. There are business men of the strictest probity and honesty, and men whose word is as good as their bond, but there are many more who will allow their conscience to lie dormant so long as they remain in the country. With them the passion is to secure money, and whether they secure it by overcharging a regular customer, selling illicit gold, or gambling at the stock exchanges is a matter of small moment. Tradesmen and shopkeepers will charge according to the apparel of the patron, and will brazenly acknowledge doing so if reminded by the one who has paid two prices for like articles the same day. Hotels charge according to the quantity of luggage the traveller carries, and boardinghouses compute your wealth before presenting their bills. Street-car fares and postage stamps alone do not fluctuate in value, but the wise man counts his change.

The experiences of an American with one large business house in the city will serve as an example of the methods of some of those who are eager to realize their ambitions. The American spent many weeks and much patience and money in securing photographs throughout the country, and took the plates to a large firm in Johannesburg for development and printing. When he returned two weeks later he was informed that the plates and prints had been delivered a week before, and neither prayers nor threats secured a different answer. Justice in the courts is slow and costly, and the American was obliged to leave the country without his property. Shortly after his departure the firm of photographers commenced selling a choice collection of new South African photographs which, curiously, were of the same scenes and persons photographed by the American.

Gambling may be more general in some

other cities, but it can not be more public. The more refined gamblers patronize the two stock exchanges, and there are but few too poor to indulge in that form of dissipation. Probably nine tenths of the inhabitants of the city travel the stock-exchange bypath to wealth or poverty. Women and boys are as much infected by the fever as mine owners and managers, and it would not be slandering the citizens to say that one fourth of the conversation heard on the streets refers to the rise and fall of stocks.

The popular gathering place in the city is the street in front of one of the stock exchanges known as "The Chains." During the session of the exchange the street is crowded with an excited throng of men, boys, and even women, all flushed with the excitement of betting on the rise and fall of mining stocks in the building. Clerks, office boys, and miners spend the lunch hour at "The Chains," either to invest their wages or to watch the market if their money is already invested. A fall in the value of stocks is of far greater moment to them than war, famine, or pestilence.

The passion for gambling is also satisfied by a giant lottery scheme known as "Sweepstakes," which has the sanction of the Government. Thousands of pounds are offered as prizes at the periodical drawings, and no true Johannesburger ever fails to secure at least one ticket for the drawing. When there are no sessions of the stock exchanges, no sweepstakes, horse races, ball games, or other usual opportunities for gambling, they will bet on the arrival of the Cape train, the length of a sermon, or the number of lashes a negro criminal can endure before fainting.

Drinking is a second diversion which occupies much of the time of the average citizen, because of the great heat and the lack of amusement. The liquor that is drunk in Johannesburg in one year would make a stream of larger proportions and far more healthier contents than the Vaal River in the dry season. It is a rare occurrence to see a man drink water unless it is concealed in brandy, and at night it is even rarer that one is seen who is not drinking. Cape Smoke, the name given to a liquor made in Cape Colony, is credited with the ability to kill a man before he has taken the glass from his lips, but the popular Uitlander beverage, brandy and soda, is even more fatal in its effects. Pure liquor is almost unobtainable, and death-dealing counterfeits from Delagoa Bay are the substitutes. Twenty-five cents for a glass of beer and fifty cents for brandy and soda are not deterrent prices where ordinary mine workers receive ten dollars a day and mine managers fifty thousand dollars a year.

Of social life there is little except such as is afforded by the clubs, of which there are several of high standing. The majority of the men left their families in their native countries on account of the severe climate, and that fact, combined with the prevalent idea that the weather is too torrid to do anything unnecessary, is responsible for Johannesburg's lack of social amenity. There are occasional dances and receptions, but they are participated in only by newcomers who have not yet fallen under the spell of the South African sun. The Sunday night's musical entertainments at the Wanderer's Club are practically the only affairs to which the average Uitlander cares to go, because he can clothe himself for comfort and be as dignified or as undignified as he pleases.

The true Johannesburger is the most independent man in the world. When he meets a native on the sidewalk he promptly kicks him into the street, and if the action is resented, bullies a Boer policeman into arresting the offender. The policeman may demur and call the Johannesburger a " Verdomde rooinek," but he will make the arrest or receive a drubbing. He may be arrested in turn, but he is ever willing and anxious to pay a fine for the privilege of beating a " dumb Dutchman," as he calls him. He pays little attention to the laws of the country, because he has not had the patience to learn what they consist of, and he rests content in knowing that his home government will rescue him through diplomatic channels if he should run counter to the laws. He cares nothing concerning the government of the city except as it interferes with or assists his own private interests, but he will take advantage of every opportunity to defy the authority of the administrators of the laws.

He despises the Boers, and continually and maliciously ridicules them on the slightest pretexts. Specially true is this of those newspapers which are the representatives of the Uitlander population. Venomous editorials against the Boer Government and people appear almost daily, and serve to widen the breach between the two classes of inhabitants. The Boer newspapers for a long time ignored the assaults of the Uitlander press, but recently they have commenced to retaliate, and the editorial war is a bitter one. An extract from the Randt Post will show the nature and depth of bitterness displayed by the two classes of newspapers:

"Though Dr. Leyds may be right, and the Johannesburg population safe in case of war, we advise that, at the first act of war on the English side, the women and children, and well-disposed persons of this town, be given twenty-four hours to leave, and then the whole place be shot down; in the event, we repeat—which God forbid!—of war coming.

"If, indeed, there must be shooting, then it will be on account of seditious words and deeds of Johannesburg agitators and the co-shareholders in Cape Town and London, and the struggle will be promoted for no other object than the possession of the gold. Well, then, let such action be taken that the perpetrators of these turbulent proceedings shall, if caught, be thrown into the deep shafts of their mines, with the *débris* of the batteries for a costly shroud, and that the whole of Johannesburg, with the exception of the Afrikander wards, be converted into a gigantic rubbish heap to serve as a mighty tombstone for the shot-down authors of a monstrous deed.

" If it be known that these valuable buildings and the lives of the wire-pullers are the price of the mines, then people will take good heed before the torch of war is set alight. Friendly talks and protests are no use with England. Let force and rough violence be opposed to the intrigues and plots of Old England, and only then will the Boer remain master."

It is on Saturday nights that the bitterness of the Uitlander population is most noticeable, since then the workers from the mines along the Randt gather in the city and discuss their grievances, which then become magnified with every additional glass of liquor. It is then that the city streets and places of amusement and entertainment are crowded with a throng that finds relaxation by abusing the Boers. The theatre audiences laugh loudest at the coarsest jests made at the expense of the Boers, and the bar-room crowds talk loudest when the Boers are the subject of discussion. The abuse continues even when the not-too-sober Uitlander, wheeled homeward at daybreak by his faithful Zulu 'ricksha boy, casts imprecations upon the Boer policeman who is guarding his property.

Johannesburg is one of the most expensive places of residence in the world. Situated in the interior of the continent, thousands of miles distant from the sources of food and supplies, it is natural that commodities should be high in price. Almost all food stuffs are carried thither from America, Europe, and Australia, and consequently the original cost is trebled by the addition of carriage and customs duties. The most common articles of food are twice as costly as in America, while such commodities as eggs, imported from Madeira, frequently are scarce at a dollar a dozen. Butter from America is fifty cents a pound, and fruits and vegetables from Cape Colony and Natal are equally high in price and frequently unobtainable. Good board can not be obtained anywhere for less than five dollars a day, while the best hotels and clubs charge thrice that amount. Rentals are exceptionally high owing to the extraordinary land values and the cost of erecting buildings. A small, brick-lined, corrugated-iron cottage of four rooms, such as a married mine-employee occupies, costs from fifty to seventy-five dollars a month, while a two-story brick house in a respectable quarter of the city rents for one hundred dollars a month.

Every object in the city is mutely expressive of a vast expenditure of money. The idea that everything—the buildings, food, horses, clothing, machinery, and all that is to be seen—has been carried across oceans and continents unconsciously associates itself with the cost that it has entailed. Four-story buildings that in New York or London would be passed without remark cause mental speculation concerning their cost, merely because it is so patent that every brick, nail, and board in them has been conveyed thousands of miles from foreign shores. Electric lights and street cars, so common in American towns, appear abnormal in the city in the veldt, and instantly suggest an outlay of great amounts of money even to the minds which are not accustomed to reducing everything to dollars and pounds.

Leaving the densely settled centre of the city, where land is worth as much as choice plots on Broadway, and wandering into the suburbs where the great mines are, the idea of cost is more firmly implanted into the mind. The huge buildings, covering acres of ground and thousands of tons of the most costly machinery, seem to be of natural origin rather than of human handiwork. It is almost beyond belief that men should be daring enough to convey hundreds of steamer loads of lumber and machinery halfway around the world at inestimable cost merely for the yellow metal that Nature has hidden so far distant from the great centres of population.

The cosmopolitanism of the city is a feature which impresses itself most indelibly upon the mind. In a half-day's stroll in the city representatives of all the peoples of the earth, with the possible exception of the American Indian, Eskimos, and South Sea islanders, will be seen variously engaged in the struggle for gold. On the floors of the stock exchanges are money barons or their agents, as energetic and sharp as their prototypes of Wall and Throckmorton Streets. These are chiefly British, French, and German. Outside, between "The Chains," are readily discernible the distinguishing features of the Americans, Afrikanders, Portuguese, Russians, Spaniards, and Italians. A few steps distant is Commissioner Street, the principal thoroughfare, where the surging throng is composed of so many different racial representatives that an analysis of it is not an easy undertaking. He is considered an expert who can name the native country of every man on the street, and if he can distinguish between an American and a Canadian he is credited with being a wise man.

In the throng is the tall, well-clothed Briton, with silk hat and frock coat, closely followed by a sparsely clad Matabele, bearing his master's account books or golf-sticks. Near them a Chinaman, in circular red-topped hat and flowing silk robes, is having a heated argument in broken English with an Irish hansom-driver. Crossing the street are two stately Arabs, in turbans and white robes, jostling easy-going Indian coolies with their canes. Bareheaded Cingalese, their long, shiny hair tied in knots and fastened down with circular combs, noiselessly gliding along, or stopping suddenly to trade Oriental jewelry for Christian's money; Malays, Turks, Egyptians, Persians, and New-Zealanders, each with his distinctive costume; Hottentots, Matabeles, Zulus, Mashonas, Basutos, and the representatives of hundreds of the other native races south of the Zambezi pass by in picturesque lack of bodily adornment.

It is an imposing array, too, for the majority of the throng is composed of moderately wealthy persons, and even in the centre of Africa wealth carries with it opportunities for display. John Chinaman will ride in a 'ricksha to his joss-house with as much conscious pride as the European or American will sit in his brougham or automobile. Money is as easily spent as made in Johannesburg, and it is a cosmopolitan habit to spend it in a manner so that everybody will know it is being spent. To make a display of some sort is necessary to the citizen's happiness. If he is not of sufficient importance to have his name in the subsidized newspapers daily he will seek notoriety by wearing a thousand pounds' worth of diamonds on the street or making astonishing bets at the race-track. In that little universe on the veldt every man tries to be superior to his neighbour in some manner that may be patent to all the city. When it is taken into consideration that almost all the contestants were among the cleverest and shrewdest men in the countries whence they came to Johannesburg, and not among the riffraff and failures, then the intensity of the race for superiority can be imagined.

Johannesburg might be named the City of Surprises. Its youthful existence has been fraught with astonishing works. It was born in a day, and one day's revolution almost ended its existence. It grew from the desert veldt into a garden of gold. Its granite residences, brick buildings, and iron and steel mills sprang from blades of grass and sprigs of weeds. It has transformed the beggar into a millionaire, and it has seen starving men in its streets. It harbours men from every nation and climate, but it is a home for few. It is far from the centre of the earth's civilization, but it has often attracted the whole world's attention. It supports its children, but by them it is cursed. Its god is in the earth upon which it rests, and its hope of future life in that which it brings forth. And all this because a man upturned the soil and called it gold.

THE END

www.ingramcontent.com/pod-product-compliance
Lightning Source LLC
Chambersburg PA
CBHW021156230426
43667CB00006B/430